Whether your daily path leads you down a rough and rocky road or guides you to green pastures, these readings be small treasures glittering you as diamonds in the dust. These gems are from God and my present to you.

To:_____

From:_____

Diamonds in the Dust
366 Sparkling Devotions
Copyright© 1994 by The Zondervan Corporation
All rights reserved

ISBN 0-310-96551-9

Excerpts taken from:
Diamonds in the Dust
366 Sparkling Devotions That Reveal the Extraordinary in the Ordinary
Copyright© 1993 by Joni Eareckson Tada

Requests for information should be addressed to:
Zondervan Publishing House
Grand Rapids, Michigan 49530

Project Editor: Jesslyn DeBoer

Printed in China

95 96 97 98 99 /❖HK/ 5 4 3 2 1

January 1

A New Thing

Forget the former things; do not dwell on the past.
See, I am doing a new thing! ISAIAH 43:18-19

His plans for you this year may outshine those
of the past. His blueprint is hot-off-the-press
and He's prepared to fill your days with reasons
to give Him praise. That's why you can begin the year
with hope and expectancy.

December 31

TAKE INVENTORY

So do not fear, for I am with you; do not be dismayed,
for I am your God. I will strengthen you and help you;
I will uphold you with my righteous right hand. ISAIAH 41:10

Lord, keep reminding me that quiet time with you
is the source of my strength. As I commit myself
to a special time of prayer and the study of your Word,
hold me to my vows. May I glorify you
in the year to come!

January 2

HEARTFELT, HONEST PRAYERS

God is spirit, and his worshipers must worship
in spirit and in truth. JOHN 4:24

The most powerful prayer I ever offered was the
shortest. After three depressing years of suicidal despair
over my paralysis, I prayed, "God if I can't die,
show me how to live, please!"

God is not looking for a lot of fancy words.
He simply wants you to approach Him in spirit
and in truth. That means heartfelt honesty.

December 30

IN GOD'S EYES

Nothing in all creation is hidden from God's sight.
Everything is uncovered and laid bare before the eyes of him
to whom we must give account. HEBREWS 4:13

Fear must never be an incentive to obey, for it will
only breed burdensome rule-keeping behavior.
Please don't fear the watchful eye of God but draw
comfort from His scrutiny into your life.
Let Him protect you, let Him guard you with His eye.

January 3

GROW IN GRACE

And we, who with unveiled faces all reflect the Lord's glory,
are being transformed into his likeness with ever-increasing glory.
II CORINTHIANS 3:18

I received a letter from an old school friend the other
day. After twenty-five years of friendship, it was good
to read that she is still growing in the Lord. But I was
especially touched with her closing salutation,
"Grow in grace."

It made me think: Just *how* have I grown
in God's grace over the last year?

December 29

THE DESERT OF SOLITUDE

But when God, who set me apart from birth and called me
by his grace, was pleased to reveal his Son in me . . . I did not consult
any man . . . but I went immediately into Arabia
and later returned to Damascus. GALATIANS 1:15-17

Distancing yourself from something that once held
your heart can be a kind of withdrawing into the desert
of solitude where desires can be purified. It's a way
of detaching your desire from the magnetic pulls
of this world in order to attach it more firmly to Christ.

January 4

EXCHANGE THE MEANING
Then the LORD said to Moses, "Raise your staff . . . "
EXODUS 14:15

It was just an ordinary stick of wood,
but when the Lord chose it for His tool,
the staff took on new ownership and meaning.

God can exchange the tragic meaning behind accidents
or injuries for something new and positive. The cross
is a good example. What was once a symbol of torture
and pain now represents hope and salvation.

December 28

GRANDMA GRACE'S BIBLE

Jesus Christ is the same yesterday and today and forever.
HEBREWS 13:8

There's nothing old or worn out about the love of God.
His love has not yellowed with age. It is neither fragile
or ragged at the edges. God's love is as current now
as it was a century ago, as fresh today as it
will be tomorrow. Today, praise the Lord that He
is the same, always loving, always merciful,
and that with Him there is no shadow of turning.

January 5

DO NOT FORGET

Only be careful, and watch yourselves closely so that you do not forget the things your eyes have seen. DEUTERONOMY 4:9

Lord, forgive me for having such a short memory of all the marvelous ways you've protected and provided for me. I thank you for all that you've done in the past and all you'll do in the future. I'm grateful to you.

December 27

AFTER CHRISTMAS

Let us fix our eyes on Jesus . . . who for the joy set before him,
endured the cross, scorning its shame, and sat down
at the right hand of the throne of God. HEBREWS 12:2

This week, aim for simplicity. The last few weeks
may have been filled with baking, shopping, concerts,
gift wrapping, and dinner parties, but today,
celebrate simplicity as you fix your eyes on Jesus.

January 6

MAGNIFICENT VISION

Magnify the LORD with me; let us exalt his name together.
PSALM 34:3

When you magnify an object under a microscope,
you don't make the object any bigger. What you
magnify is your vision. Likewise when you exalt
a king you do not pronounce him as king. He already is.
Magnifying and exalting God are functions of our vision
and humility, not of His revelation or His promotion.
He already *is* who He is.

December 26

LET US FIX OUR EYES

Let us fix our eyes on Jesus,
the author and perfecter of our faith. HEBREWS 12:2

Lord Jesus, this week people around the world heralded
your birth and celebrated your gift of love.
May the wonder of your birth remain with me
all through this day as I fix my eyes on you.
I quiet my heart, I relax my mind, I slow my pace
so that I may meditate on your love, so pure and simple.

January 7

FEED ON HIM

Whoever eats my flesh and drinks my blood remains in me,
and I in him. JOHN 6:56

The Lord Jesus wants us to know Him in an intimate
way, to realize a deep, personal union with Him.

Deep devotion to the Lord Jesus energizes service
that is tiring or rigorous. Affection for Him that is warm
and heartfelt gives boundless joy to every task.
Fervent love for Jesus takes the squeamishness
out of every duty that seems distasteful.

December 25

STEP OUTSIDE

Because there was no room for them in the inn. LUKE 2:7

What a contrast between the serene stable
and the busy inn. If only someone had taken the time
to peer out a back window, or leave the party to check
on his donkey, just think what he would have discovered!
Perhaps he would have seen the angels, the shepherds,
and yes, even the Son of God.

Come into my heart Lord Jesus,
there's room in my heart for you.

January 8

SEATED WITH CHRIST

And God raised us up with Christ and seated us with him
in the heavenly realms in Christ Jesus. EPHESIANS 2:6

There may be times when it's appropriate to go to God
as a beggar. Times when you need to seriously mourn over
some terrible transgression. But even in those times
of sorrow, God wants you to understand your glorious
position in prayer. For when you come before God
to praise and intercede, it is your privilege and pleasure to
join with Christ where He is seated at God's right hand. In
that sacred spot even a beggar becomes a child of the King.

December 24

CHRISTMAS IN THE STABLE

She wrapped him in strips of cloth
and placed him in a manger. LUKE 2:7

Wherever it is,
make time to be alone today—with Him.

Speak to my heart, Lord Jesus,
I am quiet and still before you.

January 9

SORRY, DEVIL!

The LORD said to Satan, "Very well, then, everything he has is in your hands, but on the man himself do not lay a finger." JOB 1:12

The devil is constantly looking for people he can tempt to blame God for their circumstances. But the Lord is constantly ahead of the Devil, giving His unique grace to every Christian facing unique problems.

Whatever the circumstances, they are yours and they are unique. How will you respond? And to whom will you give the glory?

December 23

WHAT CHILD IS THIS?

You will be with child and give birth to a son,
and you are to give him the name Jesus. LUKE 1:31

There are a thousand different ways to respond
to the news that a Savior has been born to deliver man
from his sins. But the fact remains that until a Child
was born, this world was cloaked in utter darkness,
abandoned, hopeless and lost. But, for unto us,
a Child is born, a Son is given! There is only
one response: Worship and joyous praise!

January 10

A SACRIFICE OF PRAISE

Through Jesus, therefore, let us continually offer to God a sacrifice of praise—the fruit of lips that confess his name. And do not forget to do good and to share with others, for with such sacrifices God is pleased. HEBREWS 13:15-16

Lord, thank you for your gift of salvation
and for your precious Son. May my lips and my hands
be ever ready to sacrifice a praise offering.

December 22

GOD'S SOVEREIGN TIMETABLE

In those days Caesar Augustus issued a decree that a census should be taken of the entire Roman world. . . . And everyone went to his own town to register. LUKE 2:1,3

Oh, help me to see, Lord, that every unpleasant circumstance in my life is, indeed, part of your wonderful design for my life. I thank you for the example of Joseph and Mary who did not complain over the inconvenience of a census, a rough road, a cold night or a crowded inn.

January 11

A HEAVENLY PERSPECTIVE

Jesus answered him,
"I tell you the truth, today you will be with me in paradise."
LUKE 23:43

My friend Debbie, a polio quadriplegic, recently died and went to be with the Lord. When she and King David, Adam and Eve, you and I (if we die before He comes), awake from our sleep, we will all think that only a flash of a moment has passed.

December 21

AT THE BREAST OF THE LORD

As a mother comforts her child, so will I comfort you;
and you will be comforted over Jerusalem. ISAIAH 66:13

He wants to remind you that His breast is a place
of comfort. In Him, you can be satisfied. You, too,
can rest peacefully knowing that Someone will always
be close to you, tending to every need. The Lord
is your father, friend, husband, and brother.
And according to Isaiah 66, He is also your mother.
He is everything to you, just as a parent is to a child.

January 12

WHEN SCRIPTURE HURTS

For the word of God is living and active. Sharper than any double-edged sword, it penetrates even to dividing soul and spirit, joints and marrow; it judges the thoughts and attitudes of the heart.

HEBREWS 4:12

You, Lord, are the judge of my thoughts and my heart. Place the sword of your Word between my soul and spirit and reveal to me today things in my life that displease you.

December 20

THINGS THAT LAST

For what is seen is temporary, but what is unseen is eternal.
II CORINTHIANS 4:18

What are the lasting things in your life this Christmas?
Are you accumulating treasured memories as you would
old family tree ornaments? Does your love for the Babe
in the manger last in your heart through the years?
Does your desire for God's Word quiet you during the
frantic rush of the holidays? When you take away all the
temporary glitter, I hope that you find real love in your
heart and in your home—that's what Christmas is all about.

January 13

A DOZEN WAYS TO BE MISERABLE . . . OR JOYFUL!

Therefore I will not keep silent; I will speak out in the anguish of my spirit, I will complain in the bitterness of my soul. JOB 7:11

There are people around you for whom misery is a way of life. The world has enough misery of its own without Christians adding to it. We are to be *in* this world, not *of* it. Do you know someone for whom misery comes naturally? Lift his sights, jar his thinking, give him hope beyond his misery by showing him at least a dozen ways to trust in the Lord of Joy.

December 19

HIS PURPOSE FOR YOU

The LORD will fulfill His purpose for me. PSALM 138:8

God always finishes what He starts. He never
begins a project only to leave it half-done.
He never writes a run-on sentence. He never walks
away from a messy workbench. Unlike us,
God never carries over items on His "To Do" list
from one eternity to the next. He always completes
what He begins. That includes you.

January 14

HUNGER

He humbled you, causing you to hunger and then feeding you with manna, which neither you nor your fathers had known, to teach you that man does not live on bread alone but on every word that comes from the mouth of the LORD. DEUTERONOMY 8:3

To hunger is to be human, but to hunger for God
is to feed on Him. Hunger and thirst after
His righteousness and feed on Him in your heart.
Taste and see that the Lord is good; it is He
who will fill you to satisfaction.

December 18

HOW GOOD AND PLEASANT
How good and pleasant it is when brothers live together in unity!
PSALM 133:1

If you are trying to resolve a conflict, it's almost worth
dropping everything else to bring about peace.
Only then can your soul—and the soul of that brother
or sister—be at rest. Unity is good. It is pleasant.
It is refreshment.

January 15

PRESCRIPTION FOR WEARINESS

Cast all your anxiety on him because he cares for you.
I PETER 5:7

When weariness or anxiety threaten to overtake you,
place your cause in the arms of Jesus.
I Peter 5:7 was a simple prescription for weariness
penned almost twenty centuries ago,
and no one has improved on it since.

December 17

TWO TREES IN THE GARDEN

And the LORD God said, "The man has now become like one of us, knowing good and evil. He must not be allowed to reach out his hand and take also from the tree of life and eat, and live forever."
GENESIS 3:22

How good and merciful of God to keep diseased
and sin-sick man from eating of the tree of life.
Had Adam and Eve done so, it's likely mankind,
in his sad and sorry state, would have lived forever.
Who wants to live forever in a body of sin and death?
Not me.

January 16

A KICK IN THE PANTS

Enlarge the place of your tent, stretch your tent curtains wide,
do not hold back; lengthen your cords, strengthen your stakes.
ISAIAH 54:2

Lord, expand my vision today. Let me see the light
of day from your perspective. Drive home the tent pegs
of hope deep and far. Stretch my life to conform
to the potential you see.

December 16

Post-Blizzard Promise

He is like the light of morning at sunrise on a cloudless morning,
like the brightness after rain that brings the grass from the earth.
II SAMUEL 23:4

There are days when my soul feels windblown,
raw and exposed—times when I'm tossed in a blustery
tempest with everything breaking loose. But the God
who brings beauty out of blizzards promises to bring
peace after the storm. And when the beauty dawns,
I hardly remember the fright of that stormy trial.

January 17

THE ENEMY'S STRATEGY

I praise you because I am fearfully and wonderfully made.
PSALM 139:14

Your body, even underneath wrinkles or fat,
and despite the ravages of illness or old age,
is made in the image of God. Your heart, mind,
hands, and feet are stamped with the imprint
of the Creator. Little wonder that the Devil
wants you to be ashamed of your body!

December 15

SERVE WHOLEHEARTEDLY

Serve wholeheartedly, as if you were serving the Lord, not men,
because you know that the Lord will reward everyone
for whatever good he does, whether he is slave or free. EPHESIANS 6:7

Lord Jesus, in your power I will serve you today!

January 18

JEREMY

Have you never read, "from the lips of children and infants
you have ordained praise." MATTHEW 21:16

Each child was given a large plastic egg and told to bring
it back the next day with something inside that showed
new life. . . . In one egg a child had placed a flower.
In another, a plastic butterfly.

"Miss Miller," Jeremy spoke up, "Aren't you going
to talk about my egg?" The teacher replied that it was
empty. "Yes, but the tomb of Jesus was empty, too."

(This story originally appeared in *Guidepost* magazine.)

December 14

SIN'S DECEITFULNESS

See to it, brothers, that none of you has a sinful, unbelieving heart
that turns away from the living God. But encourage one another
daily, as long as it is called Today, so that none of you
may be hardened by sin's deceitfulness. HEBREWS 3:12-13

Lord, forgive me when I emasculate my sin,
and make great-sounding excuses for it. I am sorry
that I try to rationalize my wrong-doing. Let me
never become hardened by sin's deceitfulness.

January 19

SUSTAINING THE WEARY

The Sovereign LORD has given me an instructed tongue,
to know the word that sustains the weary. ISAIAH 50:4

Ask God to show you today that special person who needs
a word of hope. Ask the Lord to give you His words and
then keep your eyes open through the morning and
afternoon. It may be someone who is discouraged about his
job—remind him of past successes. It may be your spouse
who feels overwhelmed with the workload—how about
an extra hug? Encouraging others costs no more than a bit
of time and effort, yet who can put a price on its value?

December 13

GOD'S OMIAGES

When he ascended on high, he lead captives in his train
and gave gifts to men. EPHESIANS 4:8

Some gifts you give because it's expected. Other gifts
are spur-of-the-moment surprises. My husband, Ken,
calls such gifts "omiages." In Japanese, it means
"a little gift which you are not required to give,
as for a special occasion." That's the way Jesus is with us.
He's not obligated to give us gifts. He owes this utterly
rebellious planet absolutely nothing, and that's why
His gifts are all the more special.

January 20

HOW MUCH WILL IT COST?

Whoever finds his life will lose it, and whoever loses his life for my sake will find it. MATTHEW 10:39

Is it worth taking up your cross, losing your life, and following the Lord? Jesus wraps His loving arms around us, reminding us, "Everyone who has left houses or brothers or sisters or father or mother or children or fields for my sake will receive a hundred times as much and will inherit eternal life" (Matthew 19:29).

December 12

HE LEADS

He calls his own sheep by name and leads them out.
When he has brought all his own, he goes on ahead of them,
and his sheep follow him because they know his voice. JOHN 10:3-4

Never is God surprised by your trials. Never docs
He push you out ahead and back you up with a dustpan
and broom. God is out in front. In fact, God totally
encompasses you, front, side and rear guard.

January 21

LAW AND LIBERTY

Now that faith has come we are no longer under the supervision of the law. GALATIANS 3:25

Picture a woman who is a servant in a house and under the law of her master whom she tries to please. She's paid a wage. She does her duty. But then, the master offers her his love and lifts her up from her place of service to be his bride and share his wealth. She may continue to do the same things, but now she does them with a different motive—love, not duty!

December 11

THE GOD WHO SEES ME
You are the God who sees me. GENESIS 16:13

When I was a teenager, rushing out of the house
to meet my friends, I would invariably be stopped
at the door by my father who'd say, "Joni, I want you
to act as though someone were always watching.
Don't forget you're an Eareckson."

. . . Someone *is* watching. Your life and mine
is an open book before the Lord.

January 22

JESUS, MY FRIEND
A friend loves at all times.
PROVERBS 17:17

Oh, the comfort of feeling safe with you, Jesus.
Thank you for inviting me to pour out my thoughts
to you in a tumble of praise and confession,
thanksgiving and petition. I praise you for being
a true friend who loves at all times.

December 10

THERE REMAINS A REST

There remains then, a Sabbath-rest for the people of God;
for anyone who enters God's rest also rests from his own work,
just as God did from his. HEBREWS 4:9-10

There's work to be done. Unsaved friends
and neighbors need to know Christ. The lost in your
community need to hear the Gospel. Whole nations
need to be evangelized. People are on the brink
of perishing and the end is fast approaching.

There will be plenty of time to rest in heaven.
Now is the time to evangelize.

January 23

THINGS ABOVE

Set your minds on things above, not on earthly things.
COLOSSIANS 3:2

It is the spiritual person who can most readily
set his heart and mind on heaven. So live in the Spirit,
walk in the Spirit, abide by the Spirit, pray in the Spirit,
and you can't help but glean a real and deep longing
for heavenly glories above.

December 9

SWEET HOUR OF PRAYER

"Simon," he said to Peter, "are you asleep?
Could you not keep watch for one hour?" MARK 14:37

Lord, you are my friend and I want to tell you
about my wants and wishes. More so, I want to hear you
share your heart with me. As I open up your Word,
speak to me. And as your Spirit opens up my heart,
may my prayer be honest and real. Lastly, tell me,
Lord, how much time I am to spend with you in prayer.

January 24

HEAVENLY CITIZENSHIP

Their mind is on earthly things. But our citizenship is in heaven.
PHILIPPIANS 3:19-20

When you realize your citizenship is in heaven,
you begin acting as a responsible citizen should.
You begin to invest wisely in relationships.
Your conversations, goals and motives become more
pure and honest. And all of this serves you well
not only in heaven, but on earth. As C.S. Lewis said,
"heavenly minded people are for earth's highest good."

December 8

I'M DYING TO KNOW . . .

Those who belong to Christ Jesus have crucified the sinful nature
with its passions and desires. GALATIANS 5:24

We say we want to know the Lord's love,
to feel His favor, to experience His joy and peace.
We want to know His presence and His smile.
But could we say we are dying to know Him?
If so, Jesus asks you to meet Him at the cross.

January 25

WHO'S STRONGER?

You, dear children, are from God and have overcome them, because the one who is in you is greater than the one who is in the world. I JOHN 4:4

Lord Jesus, I have nothing to fear knowing that you are in control. There is no accident, injury, or circumstance that can happen beyond your sovereign will. I recognize that the Devil cannot touch my life, that he cannot even tempt me without gaining your permission. Help me to realize just how great and powerful you really are!

December 7

BOLD LOVE

When Jesus reached the spot, he looked up and said to him,
"Zacchaeus, come down immediately. I must stay at your house
today." So he came down at once and welcomed him gladly.
LUKE 19:5-6

When you consider that it's the Lord of the universe
who steps up to the door of your heart and knocks
for entrance, only a fool would refuse Him entry.
Like Zacchaeus, Jesus invites Himself into your life,
bringing His own joy and welcome. And just as He did
with Zacchaeus, He tells you not to hesitate.

January 26

THE PLAN BEHIND THE CROSS

Indeed Herod and Pontius Pilate met together with the Gentiles
and the people of Israel in this city to conspire against your holy
servant Jesus, whom you anointed. They did what your power
and will had decided beforehand should happen. ACTS 4:27-28

Suppose God the Father had taken the view many modern
Christians take—the view that says that anything Satan
wants must be bad for God's people? It's the same view
that implies that if Satan wants one thing to happen,
God must want the exact opposite to happen. The result?
God would have canceled the Crucifixion.
If God had done that, none of us would be saved!

December 6

HOLD GOD TO HIS WORD

Being confident of this, that he who began a good work
in you will carry it on to completion until the day of Christ Jesus.
PHILIPPIANS 1:6

When a friend showed me Philippians 1:6, I decided
to use the verse as a lever. I would do what it said:
Be confident. So in prayer, I held God to His Word
and believed that, despite a tragic accident,
He would complete His good work in me.
And you know what? God is doing it.

January 27

There's No Place Like Home

Let the word of Christ dwell in you richly. COLOSSIANS 3:16

Home is where your heart resides. That's why
many people call heaven or the arms of Jesus, *home*.
God's Word is home, too.

God wants His Word to find a home in your heart.
For you, it can be a strong refuge, or a restful sanctuary
from a pressure-filled world.

Wherever life takes you, home can be as close
as your heart, as close as that Bible next to you.

December 5

REJOICE!

Rejoice in that day and leap for joy,
because great is your reward in heaven. LUKE 6:23

The people in Scripture were not plaster-of-paris saints
who uttered their amazements in less-than-amazing
tones. When they exclaimed surprise or excitement,
you better believe they were bursting with joy.
So when you read Scripture, never read the word
"rejoice" without a smile. Remember, God's Word
is alive and active, full of feeling and brimming
with heartfelt emotion.

January 28

EXPLANATIONS

Even to your old age and gray hairs I am he, I am he who will
sustain you. I have made you and I will carry you;
I will sustain you and I will rescue you. ISAIAH 46:4

A grocery list of biblical reasons explaining
the "whys and wherefores" behind suffering doesn't
always help when you're hurting. God wants us
to understand that He alone is the source of help and
hope. God owes us no explanations. He did enough
explaining on the cross to show that His love is
sufficient to meet each and every need.

December 4

THE WORLD, THE FLESH AND THE DEVIL

For everything in the world—the cravings of sinful man,
the lust of his eyes and the boasting of what he has and does
—comes not from the Father but from the world. I John 2:16

Lord of the Battle, please fit me for conflict today
for I constantly face temptation. Rather than lust,
I want to desire you. Instead of envy, may I be jealous
for fellowship. Instead of pride, I would rather
boast in you. Guard me and my loved ones
from the world, the flesh, and the Devil.

January 29

WORRY

Who of you by worrying can add a single hour to his life?
MATTHEW 6:27

Lord, I admit that I'm so prone to worrying about
things that happen in my life. Help me today
to trust you. Receive glory as I turn from my anxiety
and turn to you. Thank you that Jesus has given me
this solemn warning not to worry.

December 3

MERCY

Speak and act as those who are going to be judged by the law
that gives freedom, because judgment without mercy
will be shown to anyone who has not been merciful.
Mercy triumphs over judgment! JAMES 2:12-13

God did not do an about-face between the Old
and New Testament. He did not switch to a merciful
mood when He saw His Son walking among men.
Mercy is not a mood, but a changeless character
quality of God who is eternal.

January 30

GRIEVING GOD'S HEART

Against you, you only, have I sinned and done what is evil
in your sight, so that you are proved right when you speak
and justified when you judge. PSALM 51:4

We like to think of ourselves as above-average sinners,
not quite as wretched as those who commit truly ugly
offenses against God. But every disobedience is ugly,
no matter how great or small.

We will be less likely to sin once we realize
that sinful behavior breaks God's heart.
Our sins hurt God more than they hurt others.

December 2

"ALL THINGS" AS DEFINED BY PAUL

And we know that in all things God works for the good
of those who love him, who have been called
according to his purpose. ROMANS 8:28

Our problems seem to pale in light of Paul's list.
For us, "all things" might include a bad medical report,
an overdrawn bank account, a flat tire on the motorway,
or a splitting headache that lasts all morning.
Even my wheelchair seems small compared
to the constant brushes with death which Paul faced.

January 31

TAKING SIN SERIOUSLY

Have mercy on me, O God, according to your unfailing love;
according to your great compassion blot out my transgressions.

PSALM 51:1

We have a way of sweeping small sins under the carpet of
our conscience without considering how they affect God.
A spat with a friend. A slip of the tongue in gossip. A white
lie. An impatient response. An insincere word. Perhaps half
our problem is that we do not take sin seriously enough.
When we line up all of our offenses, major and minor,
against a holy God, we are then able to say with the
psalmist, "Against you, you only, have I sinned."

December 1

CHRIST IN YOU

To them God has chosen to make known among the Gentiles
the glorious riches of this mystery, which is Christ in you,
the hope of glory. COLOSSIANS 1:27

Major Ian Thomas once preached that the burning bush
is an Old Testament example of a New Testament truth:
Christ in you, the hope of glory. Just as He could have
chosen any bush, God can set any life ablaze
with Spirit-inspired power. A lowly outcast or
an honored person who is beautiful and bright. The
"you" doesn't matter. What does matter is Christ in you.

February 1

FAITH

Now faith is being sure of what we hope for
and certain of what we do not see. HEBREWS 11:1

Faith enables us to realize our true positions
as sojourners on this planet. As a friend of mine
once said, through faith we understand that we
are not physical beings having a spiritual experience,
but spiritual beings having a physical experience.

November 30

LUST

Put to death, therefore, whatever belongs to your earthly nature . . .
impurity, lust, evil desires. COLOSSIANS 3:5

Lord, I purpose to set my mind on things above,
not on earthly things. Reveal those things in my life
after which I lust, and then help me to mortify them
in my flesh. May my life reflect love, pure and truthful.

February 2

A Cure

The cords of death entangled me, the anguish of the grave came upon me; I was overcome by trouble and sorrow. Then I called on the name of the LORD: "O LORD, save me!" PSALM 116:3-4

February is the time of year when many people suffer from depression. If you are feeling slump-shouldered today, call on the name of the Lord and ask Him to deliver you. Remember, you may feel overcome by trouble and sorrow, but He has overcome the world and can rescue you.

November 29

WHERE ARE THE SIMONS?

A certain man from Cyrene, Simon, the father of Alexander and Rufus, was passing by on his way in from the country, and they forced him to carry the cross. MARK 15:21

It's interesting to note that Simon was only *passing* by and that he was *forced* to carry the cross of Christ. I like to imagine, however, the relief Jesus must have felt —after having helped so many others in so many ways, here was a man to help Him!

February 3

STEADY AS SHE GOES

Strengthen the feeble hands, steady the knees that give way;
say to those with fearful hearts, "Be strong, do not fear;
your God will come." ISAIAH 35:3-4

Lord of Joy, strengthen my feeble hands and steady
my fearful heart so that I can praise you today.
Come soon, Lord, to open the eyes of the blind,
to make the burning sands a pool,
to crown our heads with everlasting joy
and to make sorrow and sighing flee away.

November 28

SCALING THE HIGH BAR

It is God's will that you should be sanctified: that you should avoid
sexual immorality; that each of you should learn to control
his own body in a way that is holy and honorable . . . and that
in this matter no one should wrong his brother
or take advantage of him. I THESSALONIANS 4:3-5

Lord, take me now to the level of excellence you desire
for me. Lift me up. Encourage and empower me
to take these small but important steps of obedience
in order to more easily scale your high standards.

February 4

EMPOWERMENT

When this became known to the Jews and Greeks living in Ephesus, they were all seized with fear, and the name of the Lord Jesus was held in high honor. ACTS 19:17

Power is let loose when Christians start living out the Gospel on a grass roots level. As in the days of Ephesus, the Lord wants us to use this time of social unrest and political change as an unprecedented opportunity for the local church to demonstrate the power of God to change a situation, to change peoples' lives, to change a community.

November 27

THE MAJOR PROBLEM
WITH MINOR SINS

No one who lives in him keeps on sinning. No one who continues
to sin has either seen him or known him. I JOHN 3:6

That's why our battle against even minor sins
is always major. Our sin is an offense to God.
The battle may mean putting a lid on backbiting gossip.
No more flirting with your best friend's spouse.
No more saying one thing to your Christian friends
and quite another to your coworkers on the job.

February 5

WHO'S BEHIND SUFFERING?

Though he brings grief, he will show compassion, so great
is his unfailing love. For he does not willingly bring affliction
or grief to the children of men. LAMENTATIONS 3:32-33

God chooses to allow sickness for many reasons.
One of those reasons is to mold Christian character.
In this way God uses one form of evil, that is sickness,
to help remove another form of evil—personal sin.

November 26

ALL THE WRONG REASONS

The name of the LORD is a strong tower;
the righteous run to it and are safe.
PROVERBS 18:10

Whether it's silly pride or self-centered disappointment,
run to the Lord. Come to the cross for all the wrong
reasons. It is there God will redeem every impure motive.

February 6

GOD ALLOWS SUFFERING

Yours, O LORD, is the kingdom; you are exalted as head over all.
I CHRONICLES 29:11

Someone once said that Satan may power the ship
of calamity, but God steers it to serve His own purposes.
And when it comes to God's purposes, we have
His promise that nothing will be allowed in our lives
that is not for our good or that is too hard for us to bear
(Romans 8:28; I Corinthians 10:13).

November 25

THE OLD LAMPLIGHTER

You are the light of the world. MATTHEW 5:14

Every evening at dusk the lamplighter would come down
Stricker Street where Daddy lived carrying a lantern and
a pole. He would make his way back and forth across
the street, lighting each street lamp. When the lamplighter
disappeared into the twilight, you would always know
where he had been by the avenue of light left behind.

May I introduce others to you, the Light of the World,
and may their lives be touched with your glory
so that they might leave a trail of light, too.

February 7

THE TWENTY-THIRD PSALM

Even though I walk through the valley of the shadow of death,
I will fear no evil, for you are with me; your rod and your staff,
they comfort me. PSALM 23:4

Lead me, Shepherd, through the dark times. I promise
to follow you closely and to stay on the path,
to remember that your rod is with me and your staff
is there to comfort and guide. Thank you for that little
word "through" in this beautiful Psalm . . . I trust
that you will lead me to the other side of the dark times
to safety, rest, peace and joy.

November 24

BE STILL

Be still and know that I am God;
I will be exalted among the nations,
I will be exalted in the earth. PSALM 46:10

Lord, I quiet my soul before you. I am still.
I lie down in your love and open my heart and mind
to your word. My prayer, this day, is to know you
more intimately and personally.

February 8

THE BOOK OF PHILIPPIANS
I thank my God every time I remember you. PHILIPPIANS 1:3

Philippians is a thank-you letter and, because of that, Paul doesn't watch his words but writes an endless stream of joyful remembrances and encouragements. How poignant that Paul wrote his thank-you letter from a dark, stinking prison cell.

That he can say "be anxious about nothing" and "I've learned to be content" while in bruising chains makes the book of Philippians all the more joyful.

November 23

STRETCHER BEARER

Some men came, bringing to him a paralytic, carried by four of them.
Since they could not get him to Jesus because of the crowd,
they made an opening in the roof. MARK 2:3-4

A ripped-up roof certainly got Jesus' attention,
but the four friends—their faith, creativity and
commitment—probably drew more attention.
Perhaps as Jesus looked up to see crumbling tiles
dropping from the ceiling, He may have thought
of His own words, *"Whatever you did for one of the
least of these brothers of mine, you did for me."*

February 9

GIFTS ARE TO BE SHARED

Each one should use whatever gift he has received to serve others,
faithfully administering God's grace in its various forms.

I PETER 4:10

Lord, I know my gift. Let me use it.
Place me into paths of oncoming problems
or new opportunities that I might exhibit
the manifold grace of God.

November 22

A GOOD WIFE

Charm is deceptive, and beauty is fleeting;
but a woman who fears the LORD is to be praised.
PROVERBS 31:30

The fear of the Lord is the beginning of wisdom;
and it is wisdom which gives any marriage depth
and meaning. You and I may not be able to match
the work level of the Proverbs 31 woman,
but we can have her character. No matter what we *do*,
we can be faithful, supportive, sensitive, kind,
observant, creative, and loving.

February 10

THE JOY OF THE LORD
The joy of the LORD is your strength. NEHEMIAH 8:10

It is not possible to always be happy. It is possible
to always have the joy of the Lord. Some have described
it as a calm centeredness that tickles at the edges.
It's a solid assurance that laughs if given the chance.
It is unwavering confidence that can't help
but look on the bright side.

Think of all the things that make up the joy
of the Lord, and your smile can't help but last.

November 21

IT IS WELL WITH MY SOUL

Why are you downcast, O my soul? Why so disturbed within me?
Put your hope in God, for I will yet praise him,
my Savior and my God. PSALM 42:5

Lord of Hope, I place my trust in you and I praise you
for making all things well with my soul.
Please receive glory as I magnify and adore
your name, lifting my soul before you.
With you, there is no reason to be downhearted.

February 11

BETRAYAL

Simon, Simon, Satan has asked to sift you as wheat. But I have
prayed for you, Simon, that your faith may not fail. LUKE 22:31-32

Enemies of the Lord may mock Him,
agnostics may scorn Him and atheists may laugh
at Him. But only you, His friend, can betray your Lord.
In short, don't you dare. One back stabbing from the
original Judas is enough. Lean on your Lord's
intercessions for you, and that will give you
all the resource you need to love and obey.

November 20

BE THANKFUL

For although they knew God, they neither glorified him as God
nor gave thanks to him, but their thinking became futile
and their foolish hearts were darkened. ROMANS 1:21

Look around you. The blessings abound: The smiles
of children, the beauty of a glorious sunset, the comfort
of a warm bed at night. Small and great,
there are plenty of reasons to say to God, "Thank you."

February 12

SECURITY AND SIGNIFICANCE
For in him we live and move and have our being. ACTS 17:28

Christian psychologists say that good mental health
springs from two things: security and significance.
Security in *who we are* and significance in *what we do.*
Since Christ is the source of peace, joy, strength and rest,
and in Him we live and move and have our very being,
we can be secure and feel significant when we place
our trust in Jesus.

November 19

In the Potter's Hands

So I went down to the potter's house, and I saw him working at the wheel. But the pot he was shaping from the clay was marred in his hands; so the potter formed it into another pot, shaping it as seemed best to him. JEREMIAH 18:3-4

On the first anniversary of the accident, which totally paralyzed her, thirteen year-old Cathe Chermesino gave her testimony at her church. "I'm like the potter's clay," she said. "I'm being reshaped into something that I believe will be far better. What looks harmful for me will actually turn out to be good."

February 13

WHAT DOES GOD ASK OF YOU?

And now, O Israel, what does the LORD your God ask of you
but to fear the LORD your God, to walk in all his ways, to love him,
to serve the LORD your God with all your heart
and with all your soul. DEUTERONOMY 10:12

Lord, you gave your life! You ask me to do the same.
Bless you for giving me the power to love and serve you
with all my heart and soul. Take my life
and let it be consecrated, Lord, to Thee.

November 18

JESUS, SON OF MAN

For there is one God and one mediator between God and men,
the man Christ Jesus. I TIMOTHY 2:5

A man of flesh-and-blood reality. His heart
felt the sting of sympathy. His eyes glowed
with tenderness. His arms embraced. His lips smiled.
His hands touched. Jesus was male!

Thank you that, as the Son of Man, you understand
every human passion, you feel every hurt,
and you sympathize with every tear.
Oh, Jesus, may your favor of friendship rest upon me.

February 14

LOVE HAS GOT TO GROW

Love is patient, love is kind. It does not envy, it does not boast,
it is not proud. I CORINTHIANS 13:4

Love must grow. It can't stand still and it certainly cannot
go backward. Love must flourish or else it withers
and dies. In fact, growth in a relationship is very much
like growth in a tree or flower. If a flower doesn't bloom,
if a tree doesn't sprout leaves, it signals a problem.

Remember, love between you and your Lord,
like anything that lives, must grow.

November 17

PERSPECTIVE

They will soar on wings like eagles; they will run and not grow
weary, they will walk and not be faint. ISAIAH 40:31

What we need is perspective. We need to see
what birds see. When we soar on wings like eagles,
trials look extraordinarily different. When viewed
from their own level, trials look like impassable walls;
but when viewed from above, the wall appears
as a thin line, something easily overcome.

February 15

WOULD YOU LIKE TO BE HANDICAPPED?

For this people's heart has become calloused; they hardly hear with their ears, and they have closed their eyes. MATTHEW 13:15

Someone once asked me, "If you had the power, would you go back and choose your life in a wheelchair?" I can't think of anyone who desires to be paralyzed. Yet there are people who choose to be handicapped. Theirs are very serious disabilities, not physical ones, but spiritual handicaps.

November 16

IN WHOSE LIFE DO YOU LIVE?

No branch can bear fruit by itself; it must remain in the vine.
Neither can you bear fruit unless you remain in me. JOHN 15:4

In case you're feeling a little self-sufficient, remember
that in Him you live, move and have your being.
Apart from Him you can't do a thing.
So count yourself dead to sin but alive to God in Christ.

February 16

FEARLESSNESS

Pray also for me, that whenever I open my mouth,
words may be given me so that I will fearlessly make known
the mystery of the gospel. EPHESIANS 6:19

Sometimes we are fearful of not only declaring the Gospel, but of demonstrating it. Compassion may have suited our Lord, but perhaps we would rather drop coins in a Salvation Army bucket and remain at an arm's-length distance from people with real hurts.

Fear is natural for humans. Fearlessness is a supernatural grace God gives when we, like Paul, pray and ask for courage.

November 15

PARTY SPOILER

But when you are invited, take the lowest place,
so that when your host comes, he will say to you,
"Friend, move up to a better place." LUKE 14:10

Jesus always "talks out of turn," such as around banquet
tables with prominent guests of honor. Always, always
He urges some inconvenient, untimely change
in people's lives. And how are we to respond?
"He who humbles himself will be exalted."

February 17

SAYING "YES" TO JESUS

Choose for yourselves this day whom you will serve.
JOSHUA 24:15

Dear Lord, I choose you right now.
I will be faced with many challenges today,
and so in the power of your Spirit,
I say "yes" to following you each moment.

November 14

BREATH OF LIFE

Again Jesus said, "Peace be with you! As the Father has sent me, I am sending you." And with that He breathed on them and said, "Receive the Holy Spirit." JOHN 20:21-22

Sometimes when we are gripped by fear, a good prescription for peace is to pray for others. Especially others who are pressured by circumstances more confining than yours. Think of someone who needs calmness and serenity today and ask the Lord to breathe on that friend His breath of life and peace.

February 18

LOVE GOD

Love the Lord your God with all your heart and with all your soul
and with all your strength and with all your mind;
and, love your neighbor as yourself. LUKE 10:27

Be generous in your self-surrender and be eager
to throw yourself unreservedly at His feet.
Jesus is calling you to a place of intimate nearness
with Him. Don't hesitate!

November 13

OUR ADVOCATE

We have one who speaks to the Father in our defense
—Jesus Christ, the Righteous One. I JOHN 2:1

Jesus, our advocate, would be generous enough
in cancelling the debt of our sin on the cross.
But He went further. He not only paid the penalty
and cleared sin's slate, He gave us His right standing,
His goodness. When the Father looks at you,
He sees all the good things His Son has ever done.

February 19

AT A LOSS FOR WORDS

Above the expanse over their heads was what looked like a throne of sapphire, and high above on the throne was a figure like that of a man. EZEKIEL 1:26

Great and Sovereign Father, I acknowledge that your glory and majesty cannot be reduced to mere words. Yet I feel I must offer up words about how great and grand you are. Teach me to know what I cannot know and let my faith take over when words fail me.

November 12

CONSTANT TROUBLES

We are hard pressed on every side, but not crushed.

II CORINTHIANS 4:8

No trouble comes my way, Lord, that you haven't decreed. And if my troubles are constant, I acknowledge that your purpose is to have me constantly lean on you. Forgive me when I grumble at hard times that never seem to go away, and teach me to find peace in your perfect will for me. Trials may be constant, but your love is even more constant. Thank you for that.

February 20

WORD OF THE FATHER

Philip said, "Lord, show us the Father and that will be enough
for us." JOHN 14:8

The Father has placed within our hearts a yearning,
a longing for Himself, a desire to know Him and
understand what He is like. We can know God's love
when we look at the love of His Son. We can understand
something of mercy and compassion when we look
at the way Jesus demonstrated it.

November 11

WE WILL SHINE

Those who are wise will shine like the brightness of the heavens,
and those who lead many to righteousness, like the stars
for ever and ever. DANIEL 12:3

The glory of the stars that captivates you will one day
be yours. The ecstasy which enraptures your heart
at the sight of a night ablaze with twinkling lights . . .
you will one day enter into that same ecstasy.
One day you will put on glory like that.
It will be yours for ever and ever.

February 21

WHOSE SIDE ARE YOU ON?

So I say, live by the Spirit, and you will not gratify the desires of the sinful nature. GALATIANS 5:16

I think of Tug-of-War when I consider the average Christian daily experience. It's like two forces that wrench you in a fierce contest of push-and-pull —the Holy Spirit pushes you up and the flesh pulls you down. Who prevails in this contest depends on the attitude you adopt toward either side.

Remember, you can't be neutral, you can't remain in the middle. You are either walking in the Spirit or you're not.

November 10

No Dark Pews!

I have made you a light for the Gentiles, that you may
bring salvation to the ends of the earth. ACTS 13:47

There is a church in England that has no lights.
Many people who visit the church are shocked
that the architect left out something as important
as overhead lighting. But the architect had a plan.
The various families who regularly attend the church
are given their own pew, as well as a lamp and a book.
When a family comes to church, their lamp is lit.
If they are not in church, the pew is dark.

February 22

REDEFINE HAPPINESS

And we rejoice in the hope of the glory of God. Not only so,
but we also rejoice in our sufferings, because we know that suffering
produces perseverance; perseverance, character; and character, hope.
ROMANS 5:2-4

Lord of joy, will you help me redefine happiness in my
life? You promise joy in the midst of our suffering,
so please let me know your joy today as I persevere
in faithful service and as I demonstrate true commitment
in my tasks. Give me your smile, let me feel your peace
dancing in my heart. . . . That, for me, will be true joy.

November 9

GOD'S PREROGATIVE

Do not judge, or you too will be judged. For in the same way
you judge others, you will be judged, and with the measure you use,
it will be measured to you. MATTHEW 7:1-2

We must not judge rashly, assuming the worst in people.
We cannot judge unmercifully or with a spirit
of revenge. Finally, we must not jump to conclusions
and judge the hearts of others,
for it is God's prerogative to try the heart.

February 23

THE LOWLIEST SERVANT

But after me will come one who is more powerful than I,
whose sandals I am not fit to carry. MATTHEW 3:11

Jesus not only untied the sandals of His disciples
and placed them to the side, but He went further
and washed their dirty feet—a responsibility of the
lowest servant on the household totem pole.
In doing so, Jesus showed us what power there is
in sacrificial love and humble service.

November 8

GOD'S WILL FOR YOUR LIFE

Delight yourself in the LORD and he will give you
the desires of your heart. PSALM 37:4

Lord, fill me with your Spirit, sanctify me,
help me to submit and follow you when I suffer.
I can then have every confidence I'm wedged securely
in the center of your specific will.

February 24

TWO MOUNTAINS

You have not come to a mountain that can be touched
and that is burning with fire; to darkness, gloom and storm . . .
but you have come to Mt. Zion. HEBREWS 12:18,22

I once heard a sermon about two mountains. Two views of life.
One depicts a God of gloom and doom. The other represents
a God of joy and forgiveness. How often we find ourselves
living in the frightening shadows of Mt. Sinai, confronted
by our inability to live up to the demands of a Holy God,
consumed by guilt, and backsliding in despair. Don't pitch
your tent at the foot of that fearful mountain. Brush up
on your topography and walk in the direction of Zion today.

November 7

HUNGRY FOR HOME

We are looking forward to a new heaven and a new earth,
the home of righteousness. II PETER 3:13

Are you a little bone-weary of living in a sin-sick world?
Surround yourself with a few well-worn verses
about heaven or hymns about the Lord's return.
Listen to a cassette sermon on the second coming.
Daydream about unseen things and you may find
yourself hungry for the home of righteousness.

February 25

DON'T MISS THE OBVIOUS

Aware of their discussion, Jesus asked them: "Why are you talking
about having no bread? Do you still not see or understand? . . .
When I broke the five loaves for the five thousand, how many
basketfuls of pieces did you pick up?" MARK 8:17, 19

Bread of Life . . . Manna from Heaven . . .
Food for my Soul . . . I acknowledge now that you
are always with me. Please remind me—should I forget.

November 6

SUPERNATURAL ENCOURAGEMENT

He wakens me morning by morning, wakens my ear
to listen like one being taught. ISAIAH 50:4

And what does God require of you, His student?
"Listen like one being taught." That means active
listening, not passive. It means cooperating
with the Lord when He nudges you to say a kind word
to an unsuspecting friend. Folks all around you
are facing failure; you can add richness and meaning
to their lives as you offer supernatural encouragement.

February 26

CONSIDERING OTHERS

And let us consider how we may spur one another on toward love and good deeds. HEBREWS 10:24

Considering others is not the art of doing something extraordinary. It's the art of doing a common thing extraordinarily well. The most trivial action, the slightest smile, the briefest greeting may be considered a service not only to others but to God.

November 5

TRIPLE TROUBLE

Rather, as servants of God we commend ourselves in every way:
in great endurance; in troubles, hardships and distresses.
II CORINTHIANS 6:4

The pressure had gotten so strong that I was either going
to give the situation over to Him completely or allow
myself to wallow in bitterness. Faced with that ultimatum,
it helped me see clearly what a wicked course bitterness
would be. Sometimes troubles, hardships and distresses
—in three or more—back us into a corner to get us
seriously considering the lordship of Christ.

February 27

FORGIVEN AND FORGOTTEN SINS

If you, O LORD, kept a record of sins, O LORD, who could stand?
But with you there is forgiveness; therefore you are feared.
PSALM 130:3-4

Somewhere in the back of my memory, I have a list.
The list isn't long, but it contains a handful of personal
transgressions that, in my estimation, tend toward
the vile and disgusting. When we confess our sin,
we acknowledge that Christ paid the penalty for it
on the cross. In other words, He erases the list.
That's the nature of His grace.

November 4

PRESENT-AGE PROBLEMS

I consider that our present sufferings are not worth comparing with the glory that will be revealed in us. ROMANS 8:18

Consider what Paul meant by "our present sufferings." When he wrote those words, Christians weren't facing cost-of-living increases, they were counting the cost of their lives. People were living under a cruel system which got its kicks from throwing believers to lions. Talk about stress!

February 28

ME DO

The eye cannot say to the hand, "I don't need you!"
I CORINTHIANS 12:21

The first words I ever remember saying as a baby were,
"Me do!" Independence must have meant a lot to me then.

Interdependence is a wonderful kind of working
together, a depending on one another in a healthy,
Christian way. It's the only way the body of Christ
can function. "Me do" may be a proud statement
for a baby, but you won't hear me say it these days.

November 3

An Art Lesson

We know that we have come to know him
if we obey his commands. I JOHN 2:3

When I paint flowers, I must set in front of me
a fresh bouquet. That's because if a painting is to shine
with life, it must represent the real thing. If a Christian
is to shine with the light of Jesus, it will mean
taking time to get close to the real thing or,
in this case, the real Person. The closer we draw
to Him, the more our life will look, feel and be . . . real.

February 29

CATCHING UP TO OUR CALENDARS

Turn from evil and do good;
seek peace and pursue it. PSALM 34:14

Lord, my life is so hectic, and I feel that I've outrun
your will at times. Slow me down to do that which
is good in your sight. Fill my calendar
with faithful appointments.

November 2

PRAY FOR ALL THE SOULS

Therefore confess your sins to each other and pray for each other
so that you may be healed. The prayer of a righteous man
is powerful and effective. JAMES 5:16

Just think: If we turned our attention to all the souls
in need of confession, prayer and healing, it would
revitalize our churches and draw great numbers
into the kingdom.

March 1

THE GOOD FIGHT

I have fought the good fight, I have finished the race,
I have kept the faith. II TIMOTHY 4:7

The good fight of a Christian is the one battle to get rid
of all evil, especially in our lives. We choose our
weapons—either a bullet-sized verse or bulletproof
prayer. We may grieve over lost territory because
of disobedience, but we can rally to reclaim lost ground.

November 1

SHAKING THE STATUS QUO

He looked around at them in anger and, deeply distressed
at their stubborn hearts, said to the man, "Stretch out your hand."
He stretched it out, and his hand was completely restored. MARK 3:5

Lord, help me to move fellow believers beyond
the careless neglect we often show toward those in need.
Give me courage to take action against apathy,
and may your body become stronger for it.

March 2

COME BEFORE GOD IN PURITY

Say to Aaron: "For the generations to come none
of your descendants who has a defect may come near
to offer the food of his God." LEVITICUS 21:17

As part of a "royal priesthood" (I Peter 2:9),
God welcomes you into His presence, accepting you
no matter what your limitations. But when you come
before Him in worship, make certain you are not
harboring a blemish of pride or defect of impurity.

October 31

No Escape

Where can I go from your Spirit?
Where can I flee from your presence? PSALM 139:7-8

Lord, if I go up to the heavens, you are there.
If I rise on the wings of the dawn and settle on the far
side of the sea, even there your hand will guide me
and your right hand will hold me fast. There's no way
I can escape your love. . . . I praise you for that!

March 3

A Farm Road in Spring

In all your ways, acknowledge him
and he will make your paths straight. PROVERBS 3:6

On our farm in Maryland, heavy rains were great for our
furrowed fields, but disaster for the dirt road leading
from the county highway to our farmhouse. Journeying
down that farm road is much like traveling the path
ahead of you. He will make your path straight
and you will arrive in His perfect timing. But your path,
although straight, will *not* be smooth. It's direct,
but you'd better expect storms along the way.

October 30

VICTORY IS MINE

In me you may have peace. In this world you will have trouble.
But take heart! I have overcome the world. JOHN 16:33

Eric Lidell was a true athlete and a true Christian.
He followed his calling to the greatest detail,
even to the point of forfeiting a chance for the
gold medal when he refused to run on Sunday.

The victory was not Lidell's to win. Christ had said,
"I, not you Eric Lidell, have overcome the world."
In that promise, Lidell lived at peace
and won a crown brighter than any medal.

March 4

TAKE A LONGER LOOK

You will seek me and find me when you seek me with all your heart.
JEREMIAH 29:13

So often we read Scripture in a one-dimensional way,
never venturing beyond the surface. God wants
to surprise us with His Word, and so He invites us
to look longer and search harder. The more time you
spend with Him, the more you will discover. And the
more you discover, the greater your delight in Jesus.

October 29

ROMANCE VS. LOVE

This is the message you heard from the beginning:
We should love one another. I JOHN 3:11

The romance has gone out of my marriage.
Instead, there is love. Romance used to say,
"I'll do absolutely anything for you,"
but love goes a step further and says,
"Yes, and I'll prove it."

March 5

LOVE'S OPPOSITE

Having lost all sensitivity, they have given themselves
over to sensuality so as to indulge in every kind of impurity,
with a continual lust for more. EPHESIANS 4:19

Love can always wait to give, but lust can hardly wait
to get. Love is never self-seeking, but lust always places
its selfish desires first. Love is patient and kind,
but lust burns with impatience. Love does not delight
in evil but rejoices with the truth. On the other hand,
lust twists the truth and delights in whitewashing evil
to make it look acceptable.

October 28

TIRED OF SINNING?

So I find this law at work: When I want to do good, evil is right there with me. . . . What a wretched man I am! ROMANS 7:21,24

Lord, please possess me so that all my thoughts
and desires rise to you. Soothe my sorrows. Sanctify
every success. May I hate my sin as you hate it . . .
May I grow to love your law as you do. Brighten
my hope that soon there will be no more sin,
and I will at last find final completeness in you!

March 6

FOOTSTEPS

And how can they preach unless they are sent? As it is written,
"How beautiful are the feet of those who bring good news!"
ROMANS 10:15

When I think of heartwarming sounds, I recall the
sound of familiar footsteps coming down the hospital
hallway—visitors! These dear ones brought sunshine
into my room. How beautiful were the feet of those who
brought good cheer and good news. As Romans 10:15
says, I'm convinced they were sent by God Himself.

October 27

WORK AND PRAY

If a man cleanses himself from the latter, he will be an instrument
for noble purposes, made holy, useful to the Master
and prepared to do any good work. II TIMOTHY 2:21

Someone has said, "Every Christian needs a half-hour
of prayer each day, except when he is busy,
then he needs an hour." Today, cover each appointment,
each person you will encounter, with prayer.

March 7

BEYOND YOUR LIMITATIONS

But we have one who has been tempted in every way,
just as we are—yet was without sin. HEBREWS 4:15

Look closer. It says that Jesus can sympathize
with our weaknesses *in every way.* The Lord
did not share only partially in our weaknesses,
but fully. There's not an emotion with which you
wrestle that Christ has not first felt its sting.
And He did it for a reason. Jesus took on our limitations
so that you and I could break beyond them.

October 26

REASONING WITH THE LORD

"Come now, let us reason together," says the LORD. ISAIAH 1:18

Have you ever pleaded in prayer? I don't mean if you have ever wrung your hands and cried, although that is a kind of praying, too. To plead with God means to present your case, as in a court of law.

God asks us to plead with Him when He invites us to come and reason with Him in prayer. The Lord is delighted when we arrive at His Throne, having sought in advance His heart's desire in a matter.

March 8

WHAT'S IN A LOOK?

Peter replied, "Man I don't know what you're talking about!"
Just as he was speaking, the rooster crowed. The Lord turned
and looked straight at Peter. LUKE 22:60-61

The eyes can give looks that love or looks that kill.
When someone you love holds your eyes with his,
you're enraptured. But when that same person looks
at you in deep disappointment, it cuts to the core. . . .
Perhaps, for Peter, it was the look that both
loved and killed.

October 25

TEARS

For the Lamb at the center of the throne will be their shepherd; he will lead them to springs of living water. And God will wipe away every tear from their eyes. REVELATION 7:17

God gives you hope, even though you find it hard to hold back the tears. The Bible says, *"Those who sow in tears will reap with songs of joy."* That means that out of your grief, God will bring the reward of joy which will last forever.

March 9

FOREVER FRIENDS

And he determined the times set for them
and the exact places where they should live. ACTS 17:26

Father, I stand in awe at your wisdom and ways.
You could have placed me anywhere on this earth,
at any point in history, but you determined that I should
live here and now. Teach me what this means.
Show me your special design for my friends and family.
And thank you that each person you put
in my life is precious in your eyes.

October 24

HOLD LIGHTLY YOUR BLESSINGS

Cast your bread upon the waters,
for after many days you will find it again. ECCLESIASTES 11:1

Great Giver of all gifts, thank you for the blessings
of this life. Help me to hold loosely, very lightly
the gifts you bestow. Help me to hold fast to you.

March 10

THE SECRET OF CONTENTMENT

I have learned the secret of being content in any
and every situation. . . . I can do everything through him
who gives me strength. PHILIPPIANS 4:12-13

Contentment is not found in circumstances.
Contentment is found in a Person, the Lord Jesus.

Lord, there are many things I desire, but I really don't
need. Subtract my desires and keep me from adding
my own wants. Help me to find satisfaction in you
for only then will I find real and lasting contentment.

October 23

PATIENCE

Surely, O God, you have worn me out;
you have devastated my entire household. JOB 16:7

The patience of Job? I would think it should be
the patience of God. The God of Job—your God—
defends the hurting, uplifts the oppressed, and listens
to the complaints of the suffering. He may not respond
to your questions with neat, pat answers, but He
will always, always answer your questions
with His own patience.

March 11

DOUBLE STANDARDS

That man should not think he will receive anything from the Lord; he is a double-minded man unstable in all he does. JAMES 1:7-8

What we do in private deeply affects what happens in public. The man who is faithful to his wife while exercising bigotry toward his neighbor is no better than the adulterer who crusades for social justice. R. C. Sproul suggests that what God requires is morality with a capital "M," both personal and social. God calls for an ethic that is consistent.

October 22

WHEN I AWAKE

And I—in righteousness I will see your face; when I awake,
I will be satisfied with seeing your likeness. PSALM 17:15

David, the psalmist, was no stranger to the desire to die.
But his words, unlike those who promote euthanasia,
are guarded. They are carefully crafted to delete
all thoughts of death for the sake of escape . . .
There is no way I'm going to end my life sinfully
just so I can behold God. Such a thing is contradictory.
I must be righteous in my death as I am in my life.

March 12

THE PERSON GOD USES

Offer yourselves to God, as those who have been brought
from death to life; and offer the parts of your body to him
as instruments of righteousness. ROMANS 6:13

Whatever you give unreservedly to God,
He will take. Whatever God takes, He will cleanse.
What He cleanses, He fills and what He fills,
He will always use.

October 21

OAKS OF RIGHTEOUSNESS

He is like a tree planted by streams of water, which yields fruit in season and whose leaf does not wither. Whatever he does prospers.
PSALM 1:3

The leaves on almost all the trees have fallen now. Just a few hardy types are still dangling on the branches, but even these are withering fast. That's why this time of year Psalm 1 comes alive as we are reminded that, as Christians, *our* leaf does *not* wither.

March 13

NO SEA?!

Then I saw a new heaven and a new earth . . .
and there was no longer any sea. REVELATION 21:1

My desire for the new earth to include oceans
and country landscapes is so limited by my human
perceptions. Heaven won't be less than my natural
experience here on earth, it will be more.
And it will be far better!

October 20

CROWNS

For we must all appear before the judgment seat of Christ,
that each one may receive what is due him for the things done
while in the body, whether good or bad. II CORINTHIANS 5:10

Adults pooh-pooh the idea of rewards in heaven,
but children don't. Like a student before his teacher,
a child squirms in delight at the anticipation of a reward,
much less a jewelled crown of his very own.
Maybe that's why Jesus said that children
were best fit for the kingdom of heaven.

March 14

LENT

"Even now," declares the Lord, "return to me with all your heart, with fasting and weeping and mourning." JOEL 2:12

Father of all mercy, help me to understand your message to me today from Joel 2:12. And if I'm dulled to the offense of my sin, help me to "worthily lament." Bless you for . . . forgiveness!

October 19

LIP SURGERY

"Woe to me!" I cried. "I am ruined! For I am a man
of unclean lips. . . ." Then one of the seraphs flew to me
with a live coal in his hand, which he had taken with tongs
from the altar. With it he touched my mouth and said,
"See, this has touched your lips; your guilt is taken away
and your sin atoned for." ISAIAH 6:5-7

Lord, purify my words by Thy presence in my life.
Remove the dross of selfishness and pride
from these lips. Make them sing
and speak of you all my days.

March 15

A SELFISH SACRIFICE

I consider everything a loss compared to the surpassing greatness
of knowing Christ Jesus my Lord. . . . I consider them rubbish,
that I may gain Christ. PHILIPPIANS 3:8

Lord, you know what I value. You know what I count
as special in my life. Help me view everything—
my achievements and accomplishments—as rubbish
in order that I might gain you. Let your will be done
in my life that I might know you better.

October 18

I'D NEVER DO THAT!

So, if you think you are standing firm,
be careful that you don't fall! I CORINTHIANS 10:12

Lord, please subdue my corruptions and grant me
the grace to live above them. Make me realize
that I could easily fall at any time. May I lean
on your grace to deliver me from the evil in my life
of which I'm not even aware.

March 16

ME, A PHARISEE? NEVER!

For everyone who exalts himself will be humbled,
and he who humbles himself will be exalted. LUKE 18:14

Are you confident of your own righteousness?
Do you compare yourself with others to see
if you're closer to the top? Do you, like the Pharisee,
spend most of your prayer time petitioning God
about yourself? If you answer yes to any of these
questions, then it's time to swallow
the Lord's prescription: Humble yourself.

October 17

KNOW YOUR TRANSGRESSIONS

For I know my transgressions,
and my sin is always before me. PSALM 51:3

Mercy is defined as kindness in excess of what might
be expected. And for the multitude of your sins,
God has a multitude of mercies. Tender mercies they are,
compassionate kindness far in excess of what you
deserve. Where sin abounds, grace abounds. To know
your transgressions provides an opportunity to confess
and receive abundant mercy, compassionate grace.

March 17

WHAT'S IN A NAME?

That we should be called children of God! I JOHN 3:1

I'm named after my dad, "Johnny." I've always considered it a privilege to share in my dad's name because, in a way, it allowed me to share in his character and reputation; it made me a part of everything he was (and my father was very well known and respected in the community). I once read in a Bible commentary that the word "Christian" means "Little Christ." What an honor to share Christ's name!

October 16

THE DAY OF EVIL

Therefore put on the full armor of God, so that when the day
of evil comes, you may be able to stand your ground. EPHESIANS 6:13

The day of evil is when you feel like dropping the shield
of faith, unbuckling your breastplate of righteousness,
kicking off the shoes of the gospel of peace
and throwing down the sword of the Spirit.
This is the evil day.

Stand firm in the Lord!

March 18

MUSCLES OF FAITH

For this very reason, make every effort to add to your faith.
II PETER 1:5

Candy, a fellow quadriplegic, was my exercise partner in physical therapy. I remember sweating and straining all the while Candy merely played at lifting weights.

There are many Christians who, like Candy, are playing around, believing that the Christian life will just "happen" to them without any real commitment or tough obedience. As a result, they have very little power in their lives and no stamina when the hard times hit.

October 15

YOU ARE AN EAGLE

But you are a chosen people, a royal priesthood, a holy nation,
a people belonging to God, that you may declare the praises of him
who called you out of darkness into his wonderful light. I PETER 2:9

I have to confess, Lord, that sometimes I act
like an eagle in a chicken coop. But I am a child of God!
May I realize my destiny as I rise up on Spirit Wings
and focus on the immense wonder of eternity.
May I breathe in Your celestial air.

March 19

ENERGY FOR THE TASK AT HAND

Continue to work out your salvation with fear and trembling,
for it is God who works in you to will and act according to his good
purpose. PHILIPPIANS 2:12-13

Growing strong in Christ is like lifting very heavy
barbells. Trouble is, no one likes to lift them. We do
everything but actually walk up to the barbells and lift
them! When we finally wrap our hands around the task
and begin to exert force, eureka! At that point divine
energy surges through us. God's power works in us at
the moment we exercise faith for the task.

October 14

WHEN HE IS EASILY LORD

Return, faithless people; I will cure you of backsliding.
Yes, we will come to you, for you are the LORD our God.
JEREMIAH 3:22

God pointed to Himself as the cure.
In the Lord's eyes, the truly obedient person
is the one who truly longs to know Him.

March 20

FOLLOW JESUS

Then he said to them all: "If anyone would come after me, he must deny himself and take up his cross daily and follow me." LUKE 9:23

First, I want to thank you Lord Jesus for willingly taking up your cross in obedience to the Father. You could have refused it, but you didn't! Thank you for the power released through your obedience, power which enables me to take up my cross today and follow you.

October 13

THE WRITTEN CODE

But now, by dying to what once bound us, we have been released
from the law so that we serve in the new way of the Spirit,
and not in the old way of the written code. ROMANS 7:6

If you see obedience as merely a duty, it will quickly
become a burden. The letter of the Word has no saving
or sanctifying power—and human will, no matter how
strenuous, cannot give that power. So look to *Jesus*
and obey *Him* with glad, reckless joy.

March 21

THE SERVICE YOU PERFORM

Because of the service by which you have proved yourselves,
men will praise God. II CORINTHIANS 9:13

Lord, help me to go out today and spend my life
for you. Enable me to undertake some special task
for you for this refreshes and enlivens my soul.
Help me to exult in distresses of every kind,
if they but promote service to you and to others.

October 12

CAN JESUS COUNT ON YOU?

We are going up to Jerusalem, and the Son of Man will be betrayed to the chief priests and the teachers of the law. They will condemn him to death and will turn him over to the Gentiles to be mocked and flogged and crucified. MATTHEW 20:18-19

Think of all the things friends share—heart-to-heart talks, the sacrifice of time, joys and sorrows. And a friend listens when someone pours out the pain of his heart. Jesus covers His side of friendship, but what about our side? What sort of friend does He have in you?

March 22

UPS AND DOWNS

But those who marry will face many troubles in this life.
I CORINTHIANS 7:28

Marriage will always ask you to prove love.
To be married is not to be taken off of the front lines
of love, but to be plunged into the thick and thin
of the ups and downs.

October 11

PECULIAR PEOPLE

Jesus Christ, who gave himself for us to redeem us
from all wickedness and to purify for himself a people
that are his very own, eager to do what is good. TITUS 2:13-14

How people dress, the way they talk, or the fact that
like the Amish, they drive a horse and buggy
instead of a car, doesn't matter. What counts
among friends is the heartfelt hospitality, the smiles,
the singing of a hymn that warms the spirit, and the dear
embrace from a brother in Jesus who really means it.

March 23

YOUR LIFE WILL BE KNOWN FOR . . .

As far as the east is from the west, so far has he removed
our transgressions from us. PSALM 103:12

God not only wipes clean the slate of your sins when
you truly confess and repent, He goes one step further:
He credits the righteousness of Christ to you.
In heaven, your life will be known for God's goodness.

October 10

ACORNS

When you sow, you do not plant the body that will be, but just a seed . . . the splendor of the heavenly bodies is one kind, and the splendor of the earthly bodies is another. I CORINTHIANS 15:37,40

Little wonder heaven is mind boggling.
Trying to understand what our bodies will be like
in heaven is much like asking an acorn
to understand his destiny as a tree.

March 24

A CALF'S LOOK AT LIFE

Those who look to him are radiant;
their faces are never covered with shame. PSALM 34:5

On a particularly damp and windy day, hundreds of calves
were huddled outside, shoulder to hindquarter, tucked
between the fence and the barn. All except one calf.
In the face of the wind he skipped and jumped like a child.

Are you gripped with a spirit of fear? Take each fear
by the horn and lead it to the face of God. Let your fears
see the light of eternal day and you, too, will skip
and laugh, dance and sing.

October 9

LUST

If your right eye causes you to sin, gouge it out and throw it away. It is better for you to lose one part of your body than for your whole body to be thrown into hell. MATTHEW 5:29

Father, even when it comes to things that are lawful in my life, help me to limit them if I find them to be a temptation. May I walk in the Spirit so as to not fulfill the lusts of the flesh.

March 25

GIVING ALL YOU'VE GOT

I tell you the truth, this poor widow has put more into the treasury than all the others. They all gave out of their wealth; but she, out of her poverty, put in everything—all she had to live on. MARK 12:43-44

Father, when I give, may it not be according
to my power, but far beyond my power to bestow.
Help me to give out of what I do not have so that you
can miraculously multiply its abundance.

October 8

THE THOUGHT PATROL

We demolish arguments and every pretension that sets itself up against the knowledge of God, and we take captive every thought to make it obedient to Christ. II CORINTHIANS 10:5

When I catch myself, I'm aghast at how many lazy, anxious or lustful imaginations wheedle their way into my head. When they do, the "thought patrol" goes on alert and I ask myself, "What are you doing in my mind, you silly thought. You have no business thinking those things in my head, so in Jesus' name, scram!"

March 26

WRONG EXPECTATIONS

The crowds that went ahead of him and those that followed shouted,
"Hosanna to the Son of David!" MATTHEW 21:9

Do we sing our hosannas to the Most High when Palm
Sunday turns into Blue Monday? Let's not turn on God
with lackluster, half-hearted praises when He doesn't
follow through on our expectations. Let's give Jesus
praise for who He is, not what we think He ought to be.

October 7

YOU MATTER

O LORD, what is man that you care for him,
the son of man that you think of him? PSALM 144:3

The Lord's care for you does not hinge on your
hang-ups. His care for you has nothing to do with your
baggage of personal problems. You could be a wimp
when it comes to standing for the Lord, always getting
distracted by everyday pressures. It doesn't matter.
As a child of God, *you* matter. You, dear believer,
have the full force and undivided attention of eternal
Love. Love that cares with no strings attached.

March 27

YOU ARE GOD'S FRIEND IF . . .

You are my friends if you do what I command. JOHN 15:14

Perhaps you're the type who forgets appointments
or birthdays. Maybe in a group, you talk too much
or don't talk at all. Housecleaning doesn't top your
priority list. You get intimidated easily and fail to stick
up for your friends. Aren't you glad that none of these
things disqualify you from your Lord's circle of friends?

October 6

HEAVEN IN THE HERE AND NOW

But you have come to Mount Zion, to the heavenly Jerusalem,
the city of the living God. HEBREWS 12:22

The verb in this verse is . . . present tense.
That's because God wants you to have
a here-and-now excitement about heaven.

Lord, help me to see heaven
so I might live today for eternal glory.

March 28

MARY LISTENED

Then Mary took about a pint of pure nard, an expensive perfume;
she poured it on Jesus' feet and wiped his feet with her hair . . .
"It was intended that she should save this perfume for the day
of my burial." JOHN 12:3, 7

For weeks, Jesus had been telling His disciples
that He would soon be crucified and taken from them.
Judging from their confusion after His death,
it's obvious they did not listen. But one person did.
One of His followers listened, really listened
to the words of Jesus. It was Mary.

October 5

A Long Obedience

Let us not become weary in doing good, for at the proper time
we will reap a harvest if we do not give up. GALATIANS 6:9

If you're tempted to feel that your life is like a long,
boring stretch of highway, don't you dare fall asleep
at the wheel. Don't be weary in doing good,
because your heavenly destination will be worth
the long obedience.

March 29

WINTER'S END

He has made everything beautiful in its time.
He has also set eternity in the hearts of men. ECCLESIASTES 3:11

Living in Southern California, I'm longing for a change
of seasons. And just like I'm wishing for snow,
you are most likely pining for the caress of a warm,
sunny day. How good of God to make us such
"seasonal" people. We enjoy change, and having been
imprinted with the image of the Creator, we love variety.
God has set eternity in our hearts and we simply
must move forward like the changing of seasons.

October 4

FREEDOM

Now the Lord is the Spirit, and where the Spirit of the Lord is,
there is freedom. II CORINTHIANS 3:17

Lord of Liberty, thank you for setting me free
from the bondage of sin, death and the law.
Yours is the law of liberty, the law of love.
May I never abuse this precious freedom or use it
as an excuse to sin. And may I obey you
with a joyful spirit, knowing that your love
is all the motivation I need.

March 30

"YOU DID IT FOR ME"

The King will say . . .
"I was thirsty and you gave me something to drink."
MATTHEW 25:34-35

Jesus said that when we meet the needs of our neighbors,
we have ministered personally to Him.
History *can* be rewritten
—we can still give the Lord that drink.

October 3

CISTERNS AND SPRINGS

My people have committed two sins: They have forsaken me,
the spring of living water, and have dug their own cisterns,
broken cisterns that cannot hold water. JEREMIAH 2:13

A spring is a flow of water from the ground,
often a source of a stream. A cistern is a large receptacle
for storing water. Don't rely on yesterday's experiences
or last month's victories. God wants to give you fresh,
thirst-quenching life each new day.

March 31

FORSAKEN FEELINGS

About the ninth hour Jesus cried out in a loud voice,
"My God, my God, why have you forsaken me?" MATTHEW 27:46

Lord Jesus, I can't begin to imagine your agony
of feeling separated from the Father. I'm simply grateful
that you understand my feelings today. The Father may
have had to turn His back on you, but I'm glad you've
assured me that you will never leave or forsake me.

October 2

STOP AND LISTEN

A man of knowledge uses words with restraint,
and a man of understanding is even-tempered. PROVERBS 17:27

When you stop talking long enough to listen,
you learn something—only in silence can what you hear
filter from your head into your heart. Only in silence
can you hear the heartbeat of God and His still,
small voice. In quiet, you realize spiritual insights
that reach far beyond words.

April 1

JESUS' PRE-CROSS CRASH COURSE

But when he, the Spirit of truth, comes,
he will guide you into all truth. JOHN 16:13

The night before Jesus died, He spoke about vines
and branches, peace and persecution. So much packed
in to those few hours! How would the disciples
remember it all? Jesus knew their dismay. But the Lord
also knew that everything would become clear.
That's why He promised them the Holy Spirit.
The Spirit would be teacher and guide.

October 1

SPIRITUAL ACTIVITIES

The LORD said to Moses, "Speak to the entire assembly of Israel and say to them: Be holy because I, the LORD your God, am holy."
LEVITICUS 19:1-2

God wants you to understand that all life is spiritual; all of life's activities come under His domain. Everything you do can be a way of worshiping the Lord. Remember that the next time you wash dishes.

April 2

GOD STARTS WHAT HE FINISHES

I cry out to God Most High, to God,
who fulfills his purpose for me. PSALM 57:2

I am so relieved my Creator doesn't approach things
like me. God always finishes what He begins.
He completes every purpose. He fulfills every intention.
God has a long way to go in my life, and I'm grateful
that He hasn't finished with me yet.

September 30

NO ONE CARES AS JESUS CARES

Let him have all your worries and cares, for his is always thinking
about you and watching everything that concerns you.
I PETER 5:7 (THE LIVING BIBLE)

What other friend is there who thinks about you
every moment, every second of the day and night?
What other friend is so jealous for your love
and affection? What other friend forgives
seventy times seven, and then some?
Truly, no one ever cared for you as Jesus cares!

April 3

SOW IN TEARS

Those who sow in tears will reap with songs of joy. PSALM 126:5

When you hurt physically or emotionally, it's hard
to muster a patient or godly response. Pain has a way
of screaming for our undivided attention. But when you
either offer a sacrifice of praise to God in the midst
of your hurt, or respond in faith to a heartbreak
or hardship, you *are* sowing in tears. Take heart
for one day God will reward you with sheaves of joy
—all because you were faithful through tears.

September 29

A Vision for Prayer

The LORD reached out his hand and touched my mouth and said to me, "Now, I have put my words in your mouth. See, today I appoint you over nations and kingdoms to uproot and tear down, to destroy and overthrow, to build and to plant." JEREMIAH 1:9-10

The world is starving for your prayers. And the Devil is terrified of them. So don't let Satan shrivel and shrink your vision down to a size which he finds more manageable. If your heart needs to get pumped up, read Jeremiah 1:9-10 one more time and rejoice over God's vision for you to reach the world through prayer!

April 4

GETTING TO KNOW ALL OF GOD

And I pray that you, being rooted and established in love,
may have power, together with all the saints, to grasp how wide
and long and high and deep is the love of Christ, and to know this
love that surpasses knowledge—that you may be filled to the
measure of all the fullness of God. EPHESIANS 3:17-19

Lord, thank you for wanting to fill me with the fullness
of all your love. Father, Son, and Holy Spirit . . .
I worship you.

September 28

PROPHESY!

In the last days, God says, I will pour out my Spirit on all people.
Your sons and daughters will prophesy. ACTS 2:17

These are the last days. We are God's sons
and daughters. And whether you give the Gospel
to a bunch of cerebral-palsied residents at a care facility
or witness alongside Billy Graham at a gigantic crusade,
the Spirit of God rests upon you as you testify of Jesus.

April 5

THE LOVE OF CHRIST

For I am convinced that neither death nor life . . .
will be able to separate us from the love of God that is
in Christ Jesus our Lord. ROMANS 8:38-39

Human logic tells me He should turn away from me.
But nothing, absolutely nothing can separate me
from His constant outpouring of love, grace,
mercy and forgiveness.

September 27

THE POOR SHALL BE RICH

Has not God chosen those who are poor in the eyes
of the world to be rich in faith and to inherit the kingdom
he promised those who love him? JAMES 2:5

Remember, Christ willed to be born poor,
and He chose disciples who were living, for the most
part, in poverty. Christ made Himself a servant of poor
people. And He reminds us that whatever we do
to help the least of the brethren—those most poor
—we are personally ministering to Him.

April 6

THE DEAD SHALL RISE

For the Lord himself will come down from heaven,
with a loud command, with the voice of the archangel
and with the trumpet call of God, and the dead in Christ
will rise first. I THESSALONIANS 4:16

The resurrection is not something to be spiritualized
away. One day actual spirits will return to actual graves
and reunite to rise. Dead men, one day, shall live,
hallelujah!

September 26

GOD'S FRIENDS

The LORD has sought out a man after his own heart
and appointed him leader of his people. I SAMUEL 13:14

God shows no favoritism. The Gospel is open to all.
But I believe God reserves special affection
for certain people—David was one,
a man who sought after God's heart.

April 7

THE CALL TO OBEY
If you love me, you will obey what I command.
JOHN 14:15

The Lord's words in John 14:15 are not a threat.
His words are to be read as a promise: "If you love me,
that is if you make me the center of your thoughts
and do your most ordinary duties with an eye
to my glory, then you can't help but obey me
for it will be your heart's desire."

September 25

GOD GETS EMOTIONAL

Here is my servant, whom I uphold,
my chosen one in whom I delight. ISAIAH 42:1

Have you ever taken delight in someone? Maybe you've burst into laughter over an infant's first smile. Perhaps you've beamed with pride as a dear one graduates from college. Or you've felt the warmth of a loved one's gaze. To take delight in someone close means to relish in his achievements. To be captivated with his beauty and to find pleasure in the adoration and love given in return. And praise God, this is the way He feels about you!

April 8

FAITH THAT BLESSES

So those who have faith are blessed along with Abraham,
the man of faith. GALATIANS 3:9

Lord, today I want to see your hand in everything
that happens. Give me faith to believe that every gift
is from you. Help me to recognize the wonderful ways
you minister to me today. Give me eyes of faith
and I shall be blessed.

September 24

SUFFERING ACCORDING TO GOD'S WILL

So then, those who suffer according to God's will should commit themselves to their faithful Creator and continue to do good. I PETER 4:19

To commit yourself to your faithful Creator means to trust Him. To continue to do good means to obey. Trust and obey for there's no other way to be happy in Jesus.

April 9

A GOOD SOLDIER

Endure hardship with us like a good soldier of Christ Jesus.
II TIMOTHY 2:3

You can't fail. God's battle plan is perfect.
That's why you must endure hardship as a *good* soldier
of Christ Jesus. Good soldiers neither question their
commanding officer nor desert the conflict.
You've been groomed for active duty, so be strong
in the Lord and in His mighty power.
The end of the war is in sight!

September 23

SEARCHING FOR SINNERS

Suppose one of you has a hundred sheep and loses one of them.
Does he not leave the ninety-nine in the open country and go after
the lost sheep until he finds it? And when he finds it,
he joyfully puts it on his shoulders and goes home. LUKE 15:4-5

Oh Lord, this parable shows me how much you care
for the lost ones I love. Thank you, Shepherd!

April 10

CONSIDER IT PURE JOY

Consider it pure joy, my brothers, whenever you face trials
of many kinds, because you know that the testing
of your faith develops perseverance. JAMES 1:2-3

Lord, my lifetime on earth will be the only chance
I will have to prove my faith, to show you how much
I love you. When I go to heaven, the chance will be
gone. Help me to consider it pure joy to face each trial
as a glorious opportunity to be seized.

September 22

HUMILITY

Clothe yourselves with humility toward one another, because,
"God opposes the proud but gives grace to the humble."
Humble yourselves, therefore, under God's mighty hand,
that he may lift you up in due time. I PETER 5:5-6

Christian leaders best demonstrate their leadership
when they wrap around them the apron of a servant.
To lead others means to wash their feet in humility,
looking out for their interests before your own. If you
are placed in a position of leadership today—leading
your children, co-workers or friends—let your first act
toward them be one of service. Service in humility.

April 11

COMPASSION

Praise be to the God and Father of our Lord Jesus Christ, the Father of compassion and the God of all comfort. II CORINTHIANS 1:3

God doesn't want you to merely feel deeply about a person in heartbreaking circumstances. Aren't you glad that Jesus did more than just "feel bad" about your sin? He went much further than pitying our sad situation. He put himself in our place, and His love has given new meaning to the word "compassion."

September 21

GREAT AND TERRIBLE DAY OF THE LORD

The Lord is not slow in keeping his promise, as some understand slowness. He is patient with you, not wanting anyone to perish, but everyone to come to repentance. II PETER 3:9

Often I pray, "Come quickly, Lord Jesus."
But sometimes I ask the Lord to hold off a bit longer
that great and terrible day of His return, the day
of vengeance of our God. We only have a short time left
until the Day of Christ, so let's get out and proclaim
the year of the Lord's favor!

April 12

ME CRUCIFY GOD? NEVER!

The death he died, he died to sin once for all;
but the life he lives, he lives to God. ROMANS 6:10

When I was first paralyzed in the hospital, I kicked a
girlfriend out of my room and screamed, "Don't come
back!" . . . I discovered that the all-powerful God had
an odd place of vulnerability: His people, His body.
We may not be able to crucify God (really?!) but we *can*
crucify a part of His body with our cutting words.
So before you strike out at a fellow believer, remember
that anger against another is ultimately anger against God.

September 20

THE MESSIAH MANIFESTO

The Spirit of the Lord is on me, because he has anointed me
to preach good news to the poor. He has sent me to proclaim
freedom for the prisoners and recovery of sight for the blind,
to release the oppressed, to proclaim the year of the Lord's favor.
LUKE 4:18-19

Lord, I'm so grateful that when you came to earth,
you came not to destroy, but to save. You came
not to condemn wicked people, but to seek them out
in order to give them your love.

April 13

WILL GOD GIVE UP ON YOU?

Though she may forget, I will not forget you!
See, I have engraved you on the palms of my hands.
ISAIAH 49:15-16

Children can be exasperating—even children of God
—but the Lord will never forget us. He will never
give up on us. Nothing, not death nor life, nor angels
nor principalities, nor sloppy praying or half-hearted
Bible study will be able to separate us
from God's constant and abiding love.

September 19

TALKING WITH GOD

Moses said to the LORD, "O Lord, I have never been eloquent,
neither in the past nor since you have spoken to your servant.
I am slow of speech and tongue." EXODUS 4:10

Some Christians find it easier to talk to God
than with Him. But *prayer is cultivating a relationship
with the Lord of the universe.* Prayer is holding
a conversation with Him, sharing *your* hopes,
dreams and affections, as well as listening to *His* hopes
and affections. That we can talk *with* God
is truly astounding.

April 14

GOD RUSHES TO YOUR AID

In my distress I called to the LORD; I cried to my God for help.
From his temple he heard my voice . . . He parted the heavens
and came down. PSALM 18:6, 9

God is attentive to your needs as a caring father
is to his dearest son. When you send out a distress call
to the Lord, He parts the heavens to come to your
rescue. And if you need to be reminded,
read Psalm 18 in its entirety.

September 18

CRAZY MOMENTS

Your eyes will see the king in his beauty and view a land
that stretches afar. ISAIAH 33:17

It takes crazy moments, times when you almost border
on mental collapse, to force you to your knees
to seek Jesus. You then sing a hymn as tears splatter
on the hymnal pages. You pray the twenty-third Psalm
over and over until your nerves quit jangling.
Then, oh, the delicious calm that sweeps over you
when all you see is the king in his beauty
and an uncluttered landscape of peace.

April 15

BE A WITNESS
And you will be my witnesses. ACTS 1:8

Jennifer and her friends visit the same restaurant at least five times, asking that they be given the same waitress. After so many luncheons, the women become friends with the waitress and invite her to church. They have been witnessing this way for years and after visiting scores of restaurants—and as many waitresses—they have seen fifteen women come to Christ. No matter where we go or whom we meet, we can have an effective outreach for Christ in our community.

September 17

OBLIGATED TO BE LIKE US

For this reason he had to be made like his brothers in every way. . . .
Because he himself suffered when he was tempted,
he is able to help those who are being tempted. HEBREWS 2:17-18

Lord, my flesh is weak and you know it well.
I thank you that you know what it is like to live
in such flesh. And I thank you that this knowledge
channels your mercy toward me,
a sinner saved by grace.

April 16

UNLOVELY TRAITS

Hear, O LORD, and answer me, for I am poor and needy.
PSALM 86:1

Lord, I am poor and needy, for I am so often
overwhelmed by the unlovely traits in my life.
May these things drive me to you, whether it's pride,
half-heartedness, peevish temper, or impurity
in thought, word or deed. Good Lord, hear my prayer,
and in hearing, please forgive.

September 16

GOD'S ANGER

God made him who had no sin to be sin for us, so that in him
we might become the righteousness of God. II CORINTHIANS 5:21

All of our sin caused all of the Father's fury. And all
of God's wrath against you for your rebellion
was poured out on Jesus. That means God
has no more anger left for you. Only kindness,
tolerance and patience.

April 17

THE BEAUTY OF GRACE

But to each one of us grace has been given as Christ apportioned it.
EPHESIANS 4:7

Grace is what beauty looks like when it moves.
God's grace is what He looks like when He moves,
acting out His will through us. Those on whom God's
grace rests are truly . . . gracious.
They are truly beautiful.

September 15

SALT

You are the salt of the earth.
MATTHEW 5:13

Lord of the Harvest, you have chosen me for a special
task in this world. Thank you for the privilege of being
salt in order to make people around me thirsty for you.
Show me today how I can preserve all that is good
around me and how I can flavor my conversation
to make people long and look for you.

April 18

YOUR BIG-AND-SMALL WORLD

If you do away with the yoke of oppression, with the pointing finger
and malicious talk, and if you spend yourselves in behalf
of the hungry and satisfy the needs of the oppressed, then your light
will rise in the darkness, and your night will become
like the noonday. ISAIAH 58:9-10

Our world is desperate for help and hope.
But take heart: Your prayers and practical action
make a dent. A big dent in your small world,
and a small dent in our big world.

September 14

NUMBER YOUR DAYS

Teach us to number our days aright,
that we may gain a heart of wisdom. PSALM 90:12

I have this habit of numbering my days. When I wake up
in the morning, I make a point of thinking, "Lord,
this day is worth a thousand years of eternity
and that means that the people I meet, the letters I write,
the conversations I have . . . these all have value
in your sight. Teach me to measure each moment."

April 19

PRAYING WITH SCRIPTURE

"Is not my word like fire," declares the LORD,
"and like a hammer that breaks a rock in pieces?" JEREMIAH 23:29

Read portions of Scripture to prime your pump
before you pray. Let the Spirit lead you to certain verses
to use in your praise and intercessions. Then, develop
personal prayers that are enriched by those same verses.
God loves to hear His Word when you pray.
It's like speaking His language!

September 13

WE ARE MOST LIKE JESUS WHEN ...

For if you live according to the sinful nature, you will die;
but if by the Spirit you put to death the misdeeds
of the body, you will live. ROMANS 8:13

If you were to list ways we become more like Jesus,
what would you write? The following might top your list:
We become more patient. Loving. Sympathetic.
Wise. More pure. More sensitive. More discerning.
But, in fact, because Christ was sinless, we become most
like Him when we sin less. That's why a "hatred of sin"
should top the list of qualities that make us most like Christ.

April 20

SIT WHERE OTHERS SIT

I came to the exiles who lived at Tel Aviv near the Kebar River.
And there, where they were living, I sat among them
for seven days—overwhelmed. EZEKIEL 3:15

Lord, help me to get down on the level of those
who hurt today. Help me to show a little empathy
for those in need. You did it . . . Ezekiel did it . . .
And I can do it, too.

September 12

LOSING

And he said, "I tell you the truth, unless you change and become like little children, you will never enter the kingdom of heaven. Therefore, whoever humbles himself like this child is the greatest in the kingdom of heaven." MATTHEW 18:3-4

Throughout Scripture, Jesus exalts losers. Whether highlighting children or hobnobbing with prostitutes and tax collectors, as a friend once said, "Jesus rubs the salt of lostness into the sensibilities of those who are preoccupied with the sweetness of their successes."

April 21

LOVER OF MY SOUL

Show me your face, let me hear your voice; for your voice is sweet,
and your face is lovely. . . . My lover is mine and I am his.
SONG OF SONGS 2:14,16

Jesus thinks your voice of praise is sweet.
Your smile is lovely to Him. So from your heart,
tell Jesus that He is the fairest of ten thousand.
Praise Him for being altogether lovely. Let Him know
His love is better than wine. He is the Rose of Sharon,
the Lily of the Valley.

September 11

HATE . . . BUT CLING TO WHAT IS GOOD.

Love must be sincere. Hate what is evil; cling to what is good.
ROMANS 12:9

Approach problems in our society with a Romans 12:9
frame of mind. Hate what is evil. But, in prayer,
love the individuals behind those hateful issues.
As Jesus said somewhere, bless those
who persecute you and love your enemy.

April 22

THE FELLOWSHIP

I want to know Christ and the power of his resurrection
and the fellowship of sharing in his sufferings. PHILIPPIANS 3:10

The words "fellowship" and "suffering" don't look
like they fit together. One communicates comfort.
The other, pain. Yet God links these words,
insisting that our deepest fellowship with Him
can be found in the midst of suffering.

September 10

FENCES

The ox knows his master, the donkey his owner's manger,
but Israel does not know, my people do not understand. ISAIAH 1:3

God has given us boundaries in our marriage,
our friendships, and in our knowledge of evil.
There are even borders for your desires and lines
for your emotions. Stay within the boundaries
God has placed around you.

April 23

ON WINGS LIKE EAGLES

They will soar on wings like eagles; they will run and not grow weary, they will walk and not be faint. ISAIAH 40:31

Birds overcome the lower law of gravity by the higher law of flight. And what is true for birds is true for the soul. Souls that soar on wings like eagles overcome the lower law of sin and death.

September 9

DRY WASTELANDS

At noon Elijah began to taunt them. "Shout louder!" he said. "Surely he is a god! Perhaps he is deep in thought, or busy, or traveling. Maybe he is sleeping and must be awakened." I Kings 18:27

Lord, I confess I've occasionally felt the same about you. I go through dry times when I feel you're not listening or that you're busy caring for others far away.

May the dry times in my soul serve as a reminder for me to keep seeking you and keep loving you. Help me to remember that during barren times, you still seek and love me.

April 24

BUILDING ON THE FOUNDATION

For no one can lay any foundation other than the one already laid,
which is Jesus Christ. If any man builds on this foundation using
gold, silver, costly stones, wood, hay or straw . . . it will be revealed
with fire, and the fire will test the quality of each man's work.

I CORINTHIANS 3:11-13

Oh, how grateful I am that the foundation of my life
is the Lord Jesus. No fiery trial, not even the fire
of Judgment Day will destroy the solid Rock
on which I build my life.

September 8

NOT GETTING WHAT WE WANT

*My Father, if it is possible, may this cup be taken from me.
Yet not as I will, but as you will.* MATTHEW 26:39

Great things can happen when God does not give us
what we want. Even the Father did not abide
by the pleadings of His Son. In the Garden
of Gethsemane, Jesus longed to bypass the cross.

But, oh, the glorious things that happened
as a result of the Father denying the Son His request.
For one thing . . . salvation!

April 25

OLEANDERS

But each one is tempted when, by his own evil desire, he is dragged away and enticed. Then, after desire has conceived, it gives birth to sin; and sin, when it is full-grown, gives birth to death. JAMES 1:14-15

So-called beautiful thoughts are like a bouquet of oleanders on your dining room table. They may be enticing and attractive to look at, but they don't belong on your table. Never learn to accept the idea of putting something poisonous in front of you.

September 7

HEART KNOWLEDGE

I want to know Christ and the power of his resurrection
and the fellowship of sharing in his sufferings. PHILIPPIANS 3:10

Take time to participate in Jesus. Taste the Bread
of Heaven. Drink deeply of the Living Water.
Be the branch that relaxes in Him, the Vine.
Get to know Him through direct experience,
not merely through intellectual comprehension.

April 26

PLAYING FAVORITES

Have you not discriminated among yourselves
and become judges with evil thoughts? JAMES 2:4

Lord of the lost, help me not to play favorites
when I witness. May I share your love with all . . .
and with no favoritism.

September 6

GIFTS

We have different gifts, according to the grace given us.
ROMANS 12:6

When it comes to spiritual gifts, the Lord gets a charge out of picking the most unlikely, ill-equipped people for a job. You don't need a diploma in domestic engineering to exercise the gift of service, and the gift of giving does not require you to be wealthy. Giftedness works best in people whom the world would never choose to accomplish a task.

April 27

AN ENCOURAGING WORD

All men are like grass, and all their glory is like the flowers of the field. The grass withers and the flowers fall, because the breath of the LORD blows on them. Surely the people are grass. ISAIAH 40:6-7

Lord, I praise you that our sinful flesh is destined for the grave. I acknowledge that you are the only one in the universe worthy to live forever. I'm just thankful that you've given me the privilege of living forever —after this body dies!

September 5

LIMITATIONS

But he said to me, "My grace is sufficient for you, for my power
is made perfect in weakness. . . . For when I am weak,
then I am strong." II CORINTHIANS 12:9-10

Suffering has always been intimately linked
with creativity. Limitations force us to yield,
to abandon ourselves to our Creator, God.
And when we do, His creativity flows!

April 28

FAKE FRUIT ... REAL FRUIT

No branch can bear fruit by itself; it must remain in the vine.
Neither can you bear fruit unless you remain in me. JOHN 15:4

You can paint a veneer of joy and put up a facade
of self-control, but invariably you will be found out.
You can only deceive yourself and others for so long
with look-alike love and plastic peace.

Genuine fruit comes from abiding in the Vine.

September 4

BE JOYFUL IN HOPE

Be joyful in hope, patient in affliction,
faithful in prayer. ROMANS 12:12

You give me so much hope, Lord, that I can't help
but be joyful. You are the focus of my hope
and the source of my delight. Whatever I face today,
may I face it with the attitude of Romans 12:12.

April 29

THE DAYS ARE FLEETING

Precious in the sight of the LORD is the death of his saints.
PSALM 116:15

The length of our days are in your hands, O Lord.
What counts, is not how long we live but how we spend
those days. Give us wisdom to know how short,
how fleeting life really is.

September 3

ASSURANCE

Let us draw near to God with a sincere heart
in full assurance of faith. HEBREWS 10:22

My times of trial have made me assured of rich and deep
spiritual realities. The Spirit has given me conviction
that all things are, indeed, working together for good.
I am certain that I am never alone and that heaven is real.
I know full well that the smallest of good deeds done
in Christ's name will result in a powerful display
of glory. Such is the life of full assurance of faith.

April 30

A Paradox

*I form the light and create darkness, I bring prosperity
and create disaster; I, the LORD, do all these things.* ISAIAH 45:7

On one hand, God sovereignly controls even Satan's
actions. On the other hand, God is in no way a sinner
nor the author of sin. When the Bible presents us
with two truths like these which seem opposed
to one another, how are we to handle them?
How can we fit them together?

No true Christian denies any of these truths even
though human reason can't fit them together.

September 2

WHAT'S AT STAKE?

Now I want you to know, brothers, that what has happened to me
has really served to advance the gospel. PHILIPPIANS 1:12

The weather has ruined your outdoor plans.
The traffic forces you to be late for an appointment.
The electricity went out this morning in your home.
You may not be able to claim responsibility
for the situation, but you *can* be accountable
for a godly response.

May 1

SATAN SCHEMES, GOD REDEEMS

You intended to harm me, but God intended it for good
to accomplish what is now being done, the saving of many lives.

GENESIS 50:20

Satan schemed that a seventeen-year-old girl named Joni
would break her neck, hoping to ruin her life;
God allowed the broken neck in answer to her prayer
for a closer walk with Him.

September 1

EXAGGERATION

The LORD detests lying lips, but he delights in men
who are truthful. PROVERBS 12:22

Father, show me when I am not living out or speaking
forth the truth. Stop me if I begin to shade the facts
of stories or events, and help me to see that these are lies.
May Jesus, the Truth, speak through me today.

May 2

HIDE IT IN YOUR HEART

I have hidden your word in my heart that I might not sin against you. PSALM 119:11

May your word find a hiding place
in my heart, Lord Jesus.

August 31

TAKE UP THE CROSS

And anyone who does not take his cross and follow me
is not worthy of me. MATTHEW 10:38

God seems to be always pointing to one more area
of our lives that needs to come under his domain.
"Ouch," we reply, "Lord, haven't you asked enough
of me?" You can be sure that at whatever point
you resist, God will persevere.

May 3

HIS EYE IS ON THE SPARROW

Are not two sparrows sold for a penny? Yet not one of them will fall to the ground apart from the will of your Father. MATTHEW 10:29

If God takes time to keep tabs on every scruffy
sparrow—who it is, where it's going,
whether or not its needs are being met
—then surely He keeps close tabs on you.
Intimately. Personally.
And with every detail in mind.

August 30

TO LOVE OR NOT TO LOVE

He who pursues righteousness and love finds life,
prosperity and honor. PROVERBS 21:21

You come up against scores of opportunities every day
to love or not to love. You encounter hundreds of small
chances to please your friends, delight your Lord
and encourage your family. That's why love
and obedience are intimately linked
—you can't have one without the other.

May 4

GRIPPING HEARTS FOR HEAVEN

For the trumpet will sound, the dead will be raised imperishable,
and we will be changed. I CORINTHIANS 15:52

Suffering is God's way of helping us get our minds
on the hereafter. And I don't mean the "hereafter"
as a psychological crutch or an escape from reality.
God wishes to instill within each of us a strong desire
for the imperishable, for the incorruptible,
for the inheritance that never perishes, spoils or fades.

August 29

CONDITIONAL PROMISES

If you remain in me and my words remain in you,
ask whatever you wish, and it will be given you. JOHN 15:7

Certain promises have strings attached—like this one
from John 15:7. True, we may ask whatever we wish,
but Jesus qualifies our prayers with two important
conditions: We must be living in close fellowship
with Him and our requests must be in line with His will.

May 5

MORE OF HEAVEN

When the perishable has been clothed with the imperishable, and the mortal with immortality, then the same that is written will come true: "Death has been swallowed up in victory." I CORINTHIANS 15:54

Broken necks, broken homes and broken hearts crush our hopes that earthly things can satisfy. Only the promise of immortality can truly move our eyes from this world. The glorious day when "death will be swallowed up in victory" becomes our passion as we realize, once and for all, that earth can never meet our deepest longings.

August 28

A BREATHTAKING VIEW OF GRACE

From the fullness of his grace we have all received
one blessing after another. JOHN 1:16

Lord, you are too good to me. I don't deserve
even the simple pleasures of life let alone
your bountiful grace. It's too much. But teach me
how to move according to that grace.
For by it you will be glorified and I shall rejoice.

May 6

REWARDS

His master replied, "Well done, good and faithful servant! You have been faithful with a few things; I will put you in charge of many things. Come and share your master's happiness!" MATTHEW 25:21

Pain and problems do one more thing. If in our trials we are faithful, suffering wins us rich rewards in heaven. It's not so much that the resurrection will be wonderful in spite of all our pain —it will be wonderful *because* of it.

August 27

THE MEASURE OF LOVE

May our Lord Jesus Christ himself and God our Father,
who loved us and by his grace gave us eternal encouragement
and good hope, encourage your hearts and strengthen you in every
good deed and word. II THESSALONIANS 2:16-17

If love could be measured, it would be measured
by how much it gives. And the measure of the love
of God is in what, or I should say, who He gave.
He gave His Son. His life. His only begotten.

May 7

PURIFY YOURSELF

We know that when he appears, we shall be like him, for we shall see him as he is. Everyone who has this hope in him purifies himself.
I JOHN 3:2-3

Is it possible to hold onto sinful habits while
at the same time hold the nail-scarred hands of Christ?
We cannot consciously clutch sins we know
to be offensive and at the same moment express
sincere gratitude to our Savior for bearing our sins.

August 26

HARD SAYINGS OF JESUS

On hearing it, many of his disciples said, "This is a hard teaching. Who can accept it?" Aware that his disciples were grumbling about this, Jesus said to them, "Does this offend you?" JOHN 6:60-61

He encroaches, invades and infringes on your comfort zones. He tears aside the curtains of your conscience and throws open the locked doors of your bad habits. He will brashly call your sin, sin and He challenges you to leave it behind.

May 8

SHATTERED GLASS

Put your trust in the light while you have it,
so that you may become sons of light. JOHN 12:36

It's the nature of things which catch the light: The color and
dazzle of light sparkles best through things that are shattered.
Only our great God can reach down into what otherwise
would be brokenness and produce something beautiful.
Every broken dream and heart that hurts can be redeemed
by His loving, warm touch. Your life may be shattered
by sorrow, pain, or sin, but God has in mind a kaleidoscope
through which His light can shine more brilliantly.

August 25

WERE YOU THERE . . .

I have been crucified with Christ and I no longer live,
but Christ lives in me. GALATIANS 2:20

The cross is a place where one dies to self,
enjoys no rights, and grovels in humility. How odd
for our Lord to invite us to be crucified with Him;
but God knows the cross is also a place of grace,
and the nearer one draws to Calvary,
the more abundant the peace and power.

May 9

PLEASANT WORDS

The wise in heart are called discerning,
and pleasant words promote instruction. PROVERBS 16:21

Today, take a complicated situation
and with time, patience, and a smile
turn it into something positive . . .
for you and for others.

August 24

KNEELING

Come, let us bow down and worship,
let us kneel before the LORD our Maker. PSALM 95:6

On the day I receive my new body, I'm sure the Lord
will be delighted to watch me stretch glorified muscles
and dance on tiptoe. But there's something I plan to do
that will please Him more. I will kneel. To *not* move will
be my demonstration of heartfelt thanks for the grace
He gave those many years when my legs and hands
were paralyzed. It will be my sacrifice of praise.

May 10

MEMORIZING

"For my thoughts are not your thoughts,
neither are your ways my ways," declares the LORD.
ISAIAH 55:8

There's hardly a Christian who doesn't wish his thought
life were more pure. After all, the first and greatest
commandment is to love the Lord with all our . . .
mind. Memorizing God's Word is the best way
to rebuild your thoughts.

August 23

THE FOUNTAIN

On that day a fountain will be opened to the house of David
and the inhabitants of Jerusalem, to cleanse them from sin
and impurity. ZECHARIAH 13:1

Oh, to be like a child, dancing and splashing
in a fountain, relishing in the freedom and joy
of all that your love gives, Lord. Thank you
for cleansing me from sin and washing away
all my impurity. I lift my face and spread my hands
in adoration of you.

May 11

MEDITATING

If you call the Sabbath a delight and the LORD's holy day honorable,
and if you honor it by not going your own way and not doing
as you please or speaking idle words, then you will find your joy
in the LORD. ISAIAH 58:13-14

The best time to invest in memorizing Scripture
is the time that already belongs to the Lord.
The Lord's Day is a twenty-four hour period set aside
for you to spend specifically on spiritual objectives.

August 22

AN OBI OF LOVE

And over all these virtues put on love, which binds them all together
in perfect unity. COLOSSIANS 3:14

Just like a Japanese woman will put on many layers
of clothing as a part of the kimono, Paul exhorts us
to layer qualities of the Spirit. Paul then exhorts us
to bind the loose fitting kimono with an "obi" called
love. Our qualities of the Spirit need to be held together
by the relationship of the Spirit. Without that bond,
we would not reflect the unity Christ obtained for us.

May 12

Speaking His Name

These commandments that I give you today are to be upon your hearts. Impress them on your children. Talk about them when you sit at home and when you walk along the road, when you lie down and when you get up. DEUTERONOMY 6:6-7

Make me more bold, Lord Jesus, to speak openly about you. For this will not only glorify your name, but will encourage other Christians who may be more timid than me. I love the name of Jesus!

August 21

A RIDDLE MADE PLAIN

And everyone who speaks a word against the Son of Man
will be forgiven, but anyone who blasphemes
against the Holy Spirit will not be forgiven. LUKE 12:10

Once God's truth is revealed to you, ignorance
is a thing of the past. You can't play dumb. You can't say,
"I didn't know," as perhaps the soldiers who crucified
Christ could say. And this is precisely the point
of our reading today because, if the Holy Spirit
impresses truth on your heart, you *are* accountable.

May 13

BE PERSONAL

So do not fear, for I am with you; do not be dismayed,
for I am your God. I will strengthen you and help you;
I will uphold you with my righteous right hand. ISAIAH 41:10

God always uses such intimate language when He
relates to us. He paints warm images of sheltering us
under His wings, holding us in the palm of His hand,
or drawing us close to His breast. He's so personal
with us, why shouldn't we be with Him?

August 20

PRECIOUS MOMENTS
Make the most of every opportunity.
COLOSSIANS 4:5

Every morning you are handed twenty-four hours
free of charge. If you had all the money in the world,
you could not purchase a single extra hour.
So what will you do with this priceless possession?
You must use it. And don't forget:
Once it is wasted, you can't get it back.

May 14

WHY COMPARE?

When Peter saw him, he asked, "Lord, what about him?"
Jesus answered, "If I want him to remain alive until I return,
what is that to you? You must follow me." JOHN 21:21-22

Lord, your will for me is good and acceptable
and perfect. I have no need to compare myself
with others—I have your best for me!

August 19

HIS YOKE IS EASY

Come to me all you who are weary and burdened, and I will give
you rest. Take my yoke upon you and learn from me,
for I am gentle and humble in heart, and you will find rest
for your souls. For my yoke is easy and my burden is light.
MATTHEW 11:28-30

Lord, it's not my faithfulness that counts.
May I move in your love and power today
and find your yoke . . . light.

May 15

A MOTHER'S REQUEST

Then the mother of Zebedee's sons came to Jesus with her sons and, kneeling down, asked a favor of him . . . "Grant that one of these two sons of mine may sit at your right hand and the other at your left in your kingdom . . ." Jesus said to them, "You will indeed drink from my cup." MATTHEW 20:20-23

To drink of Christ's cup was to drink of His suffering. Did the mother of Zebedee's sons realize that? I doubt it. Always, a parent's desire for a child's advancement must be held in check as the mother and father pray that God's will be done in his life.

August 18

THE MEANING OF ENCOURAGEMENT

Therefore encourage one another and build each other up,
just as in fact you are doing. I THESSALONIANS 5:11

When you give encouragement to your spouse or friend,
give more than pleasant words. Take the initiative.
Be creative. Look for a way of supporting your loved
one in his or her efforts. With up-close and personal
encouragement like that, you'll be doing more than
lifting spirits, you'll be helping to build another's faith.

May 16

I'll Be Back

This same Jesus, who has been taken from you into heaven,
will come back in the same way you have seen him go into heaven.
ACTS 1:11

What if Jesus had said, "I'm going to prepare a place
for you, but you'll have to get there on your own?"
I know what I would do. I'd be like a child in the nursery
standing alone in the middle of toys and books, staring
at the door that once framed my mother. And I'd cry.

But Jesus *is* coming back. He told me so.

August 17

EXPERIENCING CHRIST

I want to know Christ and the power of his resurrection
and the fellowship of sharing in his sufferings, becoming like him
in his death, and so, somehow, to attain to the resurrection
from the dead. PHILIPPIANS 3:10-11

To experience God means to enjoy and realize,
apprehend and understand the Lord in a deep, personal
union. And, like Paul, this is *your* responsibility, too.

May 17

THE PRAYERS OF JESUS

My prayer is not for them alone. I pray also for those who will believe in me through their message, that all of them may be one, Father, just as you are in me and I am in you. JOHN 17:20-21

The entire 17th chapter of John's gospel reads like a secret recording, a word-for-word transcript of the Lord's prayer life. And guess what was on His mind? You and I!

August 16

KNOWING CHRIST

What is more, I consider everything a loss compared
to the surpassing greatness of knowing Christ Jesus my Lord,
for whose sake I have lost all things. PHILIPPIANS 3:8

Lord, I confess that I know more about you than really
know you. I don't want it to be that way. Never, never
do I want my knowledge of you to be an illusion.
Help me to consider everything a loss compared
to the surpassing greatness of knowing you.

May 18

WHO'S THE ENEMY?

Be self-controlled and alert. Your enemy the devil prowls
around like a roaring lion looking for someone to devour. I PETER 5:8

Remember who your problem person really is.
Because Christians have, in fact, only one enemy.
The enemy is not your spouse. It isn't your children
nor your friends. The Devil is your only enemy.

Remember who your support person is.
Jesus Christ is your help and shield.

August 15

NAMES OF GOD

The name of the LORD is a strong tower;
the righteous run to it and are safe. PROVERBS 18:10

Dig through Scripture to find that name of God
which best expresses your heart. He is your Rock.
The Door. A Wall of Fire. Your Bread and Water.
Your King and your Friend. Run to His Name!

May 19

WORLD-CLASS PRAYING

With your blood you purchased men for God from every tribe
and language and people and nation. REVELATION 5:9

Lord, give me a heart burden to intercede for those who
need your help and hope . . . whether it's across
the street, or around the world.

August 14

THE POWER OF GOD

I pray also that the eyes of your heart may be enlightened
in order that you may know the hope to which he has called you,
the riches of his glorious inheritance in the saints, and his
incomparably great power for us who believe. That power is like
the working of his mighty strength, which he exerted in Christ
when he raised him from the dead. EPHESIANS 1:18-20

It takes God's power to be a faithful spouse,
a conscientious parent, or a responsible office worker.
If you're struggling, remember that His power for you
is incomparably great. If the Father could raise His Son
from the dead, He can raise you above your circumstances.

May 20

Hearts Fully Committed

But your hearts must be fully committed
to the LORD our God, to live by his decrees
and obey his commands, as at this time. I KINGS 8:61

Lord, give me an undivided heart that is wholly devoted
to you. Please unite my heart to fear your name,
and may I not turn to the right or to the left
but set my face like a flint. Help me to live life straight
ahead. Help me to pay attention. Arm me against
devilish distractions. Let me be singlehearted
and fully committed to you.

August 13

STRENGTH TO STRENGTH

Blessed are those whose strength is in you, who have set
their hearts on pilgrimage.... They go from strength to strength
till each appears before God in Zion. PSALM 84:5-7

Remind me, Lord, to take many pauses throughout
the day to think about you, pray to you, share a verse
of Scripture with a friend or sing a hymn even if no one's
around. Carry me from strength to strength.

May 21

LIVING SACRIFICES

Therefore, I urge you, brothers, in view of God's mercy,
to offer your bodies as living sacrifices, holy and pleasing to God
—this is your spiritual act of worship. ROMANS 12:1

If presenting yourself as a living sacrifice seems
downright distasteful, if you find yourself trying
to devise a way of serving God that seems more
agreeable to your comforts, remember this:
Jesus sacrificed everything for you.

August 12

HYSSOP

Cleanse me with hyssop, and I will be clean.
PSALM 51:7

I used to think that the intense and constant pain I felt over sin was a kind of punishment from God, a display of His wrath. But not so. Remorse over personal sin is the sign of a softened conscience. A conscience that is sensitive—sometimes hypersensitive—to evil. Such pain is a prologue to God's favor.

May 22

No Longer a Slave to Sin

For we know that our old self was crucified with him
so that the body of sin might be rendered powerless,
that we should no longer be slaves to sin—because anyone
who has died has been freed from sin. ROMANS 6:6-7

Lord, thank you that through your death,
my old sin-loving nature was mortally wounded.
I no longer have to sin! I have power to say no
because I place my faith in you and consider myself
alive to God!

August 11

FINDING GOD'S WILL

Be joyful always; pray continually; give thanks
in all circumstances, for this is God's will for you in Christ Jesus.
I THESSALONIANS 5:16-18

There's hardly a Christian who hasn't looked
into the future and questioned, "What is God's will
for my life?" Today's verse may be short and sweet,
but it's all the answer you need. Be joyful.
Pray continually. Give thanks.
For *this* is God's will for you in Christ Jesus.

May 23

DEAD TO SIN . . . ALIVE TO GOD

What shall we say, then? Shall we go on sinning so that grace
may increase? By no means! We died to sin;
how can we live in it any longer? ROMANS 6:1-2

I can hear you saying, "But that's impossible.
We may be Christians, but we're still human beings
and sin is a fact of life." Yes, I agree that sin is a fact
of life. Sin's presence is still everywhere, tempting
and enticing us. But does sin have to be our master?
No! Never! We are free of its power.

August 10

STUDYING SCRIPTURE

You diligently study the Scriptures because you think that by them you possess eternal life. These are the Scriptures that testify about me, yet you refuse to come to me to have life. JOHN 5:39-40

Always ask the Spirit of God to illumine the Word to you. Otherwise, your study could end up a dry, intellectual exercise. God's Spirit is the one who makes Jesus, the Truth, come alive through the truth of the Word.

May 24

Being Clothed

For the perishable must clothe itself with the imperishable,
and the mortal with immortality. I CORINTHIANS 15:53

The best way to guarantee being clothed
with righteousness in heaven, is to clothe ourselves
with godly attributes down here on earth.

August 9

So You're Exhausted?

When Jesus landed and saw a large crowd, he had compassion on them and healed their sick. As evening approached, the disciples came to find him and said, "This is a remote place, and it's already getting late. Send the crowds away, so they can go to the villages and buy themselves some food." Jesus replied, "They do not need to go away." MATTHEW 14:14-16

The love of Jesus can never be exhausted.

May 25

SHARING IN GOD'S NATURE

He has given us his very great and precious promises, so that through them you may participate in the divine nature and escape the corruption in the world caused by evil desires. II PETER 1:4

Those who receive the promises of the Gospel are renewed in the spirit of their mind, after the image of God—in knowledge, righteousness and holiness. Their hearts are set for God and His service and they have a heavenly disposition in their soul. This is what it means to participate in His divine nature.

August 8

MAPS

Whether you turn to the right or to the left, your ears will hear a voice behind you, saying, "This is the way; walk in it." ISAIAH 30:21

Lord Jesus, you are the Way and I know
that no matter what lies ahead today, I am safe
and secure when I keep close to you. Thank you
for being my guide and my map. Your Word tells me
exactly where I'm going and how to get there.
I love following you!

May 26

THE RIGHT WAY TO RUN A RACE

We who are strong ought to bear with the failings of the weak and not to please ourselves. Each of us should please his neighbor for his good, to build him up. ROMANS 15:1-2

We must run the race not to please ourselves, but to please the Lord. That often means taking time to stop and put our arms around a weaker friend who needs to get back on track.

August 7

WHAT'S FAIR?

Who has understood the mind of the LORD, or instructed him as his counselor? Whom did the LORD consult to enlighten him, and who taught him the right way? ISAIAH 40:13-14

The "fairness doctrine" is based on a person's limited value system and timetable. Remember, God is not fair—He is just. He is loving. His values are higher, far exalted above yours. His timetable is different. So bow to His justice, trust in His love and forget about fairness.

May 27

BODY BUILDING

From him the whole body, joined and held together
by every supporting ligament, grows and builds itself up in love,
as each part does its work. EPHESIANS 4:16

One of the best things we can do for our brothers
and sisters in Christ is to gain victory in our trials.
We affect one another spiritually by what we are
and do individually.

Help me to remember that my perseverance
and joy will profoundly influence the lives
of others who observe me today.

August 6

FOR THOSE WHO SEARCH

It is the glory of God to conceal a matter.
PROVERBS 25:2

To those who draw closest to the Lord, to those who
desire His intimate company, Jesus says, "The secret of the
kingdom of God has been given to you" (Mark 4:11).
If you sit at His feet, full of awe and wonder, He will draw
you into His confidence, unraveling His innermost
thoughts and heartfelt hopes, voicing His desires
for you and for the rest of those who search.

May 28

THE IRONY OF GOD

"Not by might nor by power, but by my Spirit,"
says the LORD Almighty. ZECHARIAH 4:6

God delights in showing up His power through weak
and unlikely people. He specializes in irony,
always choosing a combination of circumstances
opposite of what one might expect to get the job done.
There are plenty of ironies in your life and each one
is a reason to give God praise. His power always
is best displayed through weakness.

August 5

HE SATISFIES

You open your hand and satisfy the desires
of every living thing. PSALM 145:16

There's nothing quite like the satisfaction of a glass of cold,
spring water on a hot August afternoon. A cold shower
after mowing the lawn. Being satisfied means you've been
filled, you want nothing more and that the thirsty longing
has been quenched. That's exactly how Jesus satisfies.
To have Him means that you have it all. To trust Him
means that your needs are met. To know Him is to realize
that He is your dearest, most faithful companion.

May 29

GETTING RID OF FEAR

So that by his death he might destroy him who holds the power of death—that is, the devil—and free those who all their lives were held in slavery by their fear of death. HEBREWS 2:14-15

Prince of Peace, forgive me for allowing fear
to come between us. I have no need to fear
what will happen today. I have no need to fear
what will happen when I die. Free me to live
every day without fear.

August 4

TIMELESS MOMENTS

Be very careful, then, how you live—not as unwise but as wise,
making the most of every opportunity, because the days are evil.
EPHESIANS 5:15-16

Like a sunset, life will soon be over in a flash.
All the color and glory that we now enjoy will one day
suddenly vanish. That's why we must weigh the hours
presently and realize there are timeless moments to be
lived right now. A smile for the gas station attendant.
A pleasant "God bless you" for the woman at the
market. A hug for your spouse, straight from the heart.

May 30

MEMORIES

He has told us that you always have pleasant memories of us
and that you long to see us, just as we also long to see you.

I THESSALONIANS 3:6

Warm and lovely memories have a way of helping you
live life better in the present. Think of the embrace
of the friend who led you to Jesus. Recall the time
in church when you cried as you sang a favorite hymn.
Think back on a prayer meeting when the intercessions
flowed so easily that you felt you could have prayed
forever. Pick out a memory . . . and savor the sweetness.

August 3

GOD'S PLAN FOR YOU

"For I know the plans I have for you," declares the LORD,
"plans to prosper you and not to harm you,
plans to give you hope and a future." JEREMIAH 29:11

God will only permit in your life those trials that,
with His grace, you are able to handle. That includes
everything from emotional pain to physical paralysis.
And this is why you have the assurance
that His plans only mean spiritual prosperity
for you and a hopeful future.

May 31

FLOWERS FROM AFFLICTION

It was good for me to be afflicted
so that I might learn your decrees. PSALM 119:71

Just as flower bulbs need the nipping frost
to revive and blossom, hardships have a way of helping
peace and joy blossom in your life. Patience can flower
out of failure, and self-control
or kindness can bud out of brokenness.

August 2

GOD FULFILLS HIS PURPOSE

I cry out to God Most High, to God,
who fulfills his purpose
for me. PSALM 57:2

God *will* fulfill His purpose for you. He'll do it
for you because He keeps His promise.
He'll fulfill His plan *in* you by creating in you
the image of His Son. Also, God will fulfill
His plan *through* you as you touch others
with His love and faithfulness.

June 1

LET GO AND LET GOD?

Then the LORD said to Moses, "Why are you crying out to me?
Tell the Israelites to move on." EXODUS 14:15

If danger is about, if temptation is knocking,
if a friend needs help, if the Devil is gearing up
for an attack, God does not want His people
to stand still. "Letting go and letting God" speaks
to only half the battle. The other half involves you
moving forward in His power.

August 1

CHANGING THE SUBJECT

Blessed is the man who will eat at the feast
in the kingdom of God. LUKE 14:15

Almighty God, I know I've often tried to change
the spiritual subject when I've sensed your conviction
in my heart. When you've pricked my conscience,
I've often tried to divert your attention to other areas
of my life. May I listen to you today
and not try to change the subject
when your Word speaks loud and clear.

June 2

SITTING . . . CARRYING

Do not merely listen to the word, and so deceive yourselves.
Do what it says. JAMES 1:22

Jesus, my Teacher and Healer, I don't want to be like
the Pharisees who were very good at sitting and
listening; I want to be like the four friends who carried
the paralyzed man. When I see a person in need today,
inspire me to believe and take action. Help me
to carry his burden and, in so doing,
together we will glorify you.

July 31

SPIRITUAL WARFARE

He who overcomes will inherit all this,
and I will be his God and he will be my son. REVELATION 21:7

Spiritual warfare against the world, the flesh
and the Devil is one long continuous struggle.
God's battle plan can't fail, and the medal of honor,
for those who overcome, is holiness.

June 3

CROWN OF SPLENDOR

Gray hair is a crown of splendor;
it is attained by a righteous life. PROVERBS 16:31

How grateful we can be to elderly saints
who make prayer a life vocation. One day eternity
shall reveal how far and wide Christ's Gospel
was advanced through the faithful prayers
of old and faithful Christians.

July 30

HONESTY IN HEART

Above all else, guard your heart, for it is the wellspring of life.
PROVERBS 4:23

Since your heart is the wellspring of your life, the Devil
will pull out all the stops to prevent you from being
honest in heart. He does not mind your behavior
being blameless and upright in human eyes as long as
your heart remains self-consumed before God.
Self-conscious. Self-absorbed. Self-indulgent.
Self-pitying. Self-aware. Self-centered.

June 4

FOR GOD SO LOVED THE WORLD

For God so loved the world that he gave
his one and only Son. JOHN 3:16

Oh Lord, there isn't a pain I endure or a disappointment
I face that you haven't already overcome.
Thank you that you fully and completely understand
my fears and frustrations, my hurt and weakness.
Thank you for loving the world so much that you
would give your one and only Son . . .
this is enough to calm my hurts.

July 29

TRIALS AND TEMPTATIONS

Blessed is the man who perseveres under trial, because when he has stood the test, he will receive the crown of life that God has promised to those who love him. When tempted, no one should say, "God is tempting me." For God cannot be tempted by evil, nor does he tempt anyone. JAMES 1:12-13

A trial is a test God puts before us to prove our faith and produce perseverance. Trials are something we can face with joy. There's nothing joyful about temptation. Temptations occur when we are enticed and dragged away by our own evil desire.

June 5

THE HEART OF JESUS

Though he brings grief, he will show compassion, so great
is his unfailing love. For he does not willingly bring affliction
or grief to the children of men. LAMENTATIONS 3:32-33

He does not *willingly,* or that is, *from the heart* bring
affliction or grief. Suffering may be a part of God's
larger and most mysterious plan, but God's intention
is always to demonstrate compassion and unfailing love
which touches people at their deepest point of need.

July 28

MEEKNESS

Blessed are the meek, for they will inherit the earth.
MATTHEW 5:5

Lord, you willingly yielded your rights to the Father
and became the most meek and humble man
who ever lived. Help me to humble myself
before you as I give you my time,
my possessions . . . my life.

June 6

GET READY

Listen, I tell you a mystery: We will not all sleep, but we will
all be changed. Therefore, my dear brothers, stand firm.
Let nothing move you. I CORINTHIANS 15:51,58

Lord, I can spend many moments speculating
what heaven will be like, but I need your prodding
to keep me strong and to keep me working
in your service down here on earth.

July 27

SALVATION'S DIRTY WORK

It is the blood that makes atonement for one's life.
LEVITICUS 17:11

The shedding of blood is the "dirty work" of salvation.
Just as there was nothing pretty about Old Testament
sacrifices, the shedding of blood sealing the
New Covenant was just as offensive. The brutal
crucifixion of Christ was not hidden from the view
of men, but on a hill in broad daylight for all to see.

June 7

BODY PARTS

Now you are the body of Christ, and each one of you is a part of it.

I CORINTHIANS 12:27

Someone needs you today. You could be the hands
or the ears or the voice of someone who needs help.
We're in this together so find a part of the body
that can't be complete without you.

July 26

GLORY

I am the LORD; that is my name! I will not give my glory
to another or my praise to idols. ISAIAH 42:8

Although glory is God's and God's alone,
He has told us in I Peter 5:1 that one day
we will share in the glory to be revealed.

Thank you for that indescribable gift.
Until that day, I glory and boast in you, and you alone.

June 8

HOUSEBROKEN SINS

Therefore, since we are surrounded by such a great cloud
of witnesses, let us throw off everything that hinders and the sin
that so easily entangles, and let us run with perseverance the race
marked out for us. HEBREWS 12:1

What sins have you housebroken? What secret, small
transgression have you tamed to make your own?
A private fantasy? A daydream you've shielded
against the scrutiny of the Spirit?

July 25

VENGEANCE

Do not take revenge, my friends, but leave room for God's wrath,
for it is written; "It is mine to avenge; I will repay," says the Lord.
ROMANS 12:19

How wonderful to think, though, that one day
on the other side of eternity, we who are saints
will judge the world with the Lord Jesus
(I Corinthians 6:2). Until that time,
leave in God's hands what is rightfully his.
Vengeance is the Lord's, not yours.

June 9

COBWEB PROBLEMS

For our light and momentary troubles are achieving for us
an eternal glory that far outweighs them all. II CORINTHIANS 4:17

Wouldn't it be glorious if we could consider all our trials
to be as light and momentary as cobwebs?
We can! Whatever troubles are weighing you down
—doubt or anxiety, insecurity or fears—they are
not chains. They are featherweight when compared
to the glory yet to come.

July 24

NEAR THE CROSS

When Jesus had again crossed over by boat to the other side
of the lake, a large crowd gathered around him. MARK 5:21

There was plenty of room near the cross.
Too much room.

Sadly, it's true today. Many Christians are satisfied to
remain at a safe distance from the cross.
Yet if we are to see real and lasting change
in our lives, if we are to reckon ourselves dead to sin, it
requires keeping near the cross.

June 10

TRUE SERVICE

Whatever you do, work at it with all your heart,
as working for the Lord, not for men. COLOSSIANS 3:23

When our focus in Christian service is squarely
on the Lord Jesus, our work may be tiring,
but it doesn't have to be tiresome. We may get weary,
but our work does not have to be wearisome
if our energy comes directly from the Lord Jesus.
How can service to the Lord be a tedious, boring effort?

July 23

SMILE, GOD LIKES YOU

For the LORD takes delight in his people;
he crowns the humble with salvation. PSALM 149:4

Lord, I've never considered your affection and desire
for my company. I've been busy assuming
that your face has been in an eternal scowl
since Adam sinned. But now I know you love me
and are pleased with me. May I live joyfully
knowing such pleasure.

June 11

HIDDEN SINS

For whatever is hidden is meant to be disclosed, and whatever
is concealed is meant to be brought out into the open. MARK 4:22

Hypocrisy is a hard game to play because it is one
deceiver against many observers. A hypocrite will
always be found out. Secret sinning, although an easier
game to play, is far more deadly. Hidden sins
can be concealed, and, for that reason,
are far more damaging to your character.

July 22

EVERYTHING . . . OR SOME THINGS?

In him we were also chosen having been predestined according
to the plan of him who works out everything in conformity
with the purpose of his will. EPHESIANS 1:11

You are *not* the brunt of some divine cruel joke
where it concerns problems in your life.
Just knowing God works out everything
—not just some things—for His purpose
can shore up peace and hope.

June 12

A RED FLAG!

Seek the LORD while he may be found; call on him while he is near.
Let the wicked forsake his way and the evil man his thoughts.
ISAIAH 55:6-7

Lord, I never want to lose my sensitivity to sin.
I repent of my transgressions, great and small.
I turn the other way and seek your face.
Thank you for being near!

July 21

INFINITE LOVE

God is love. Whoever lives in love lives in God,
and God in him. I JOHN 4:16

Remember, God's love may be divided up for an infinite
number of people on earth, but because His love
is eternal and without end, He can still infinitely
pour out His love on you. Just for you.

June 13

PLEASURE

You have made known to me the path of life; you will fill me
with joy in your presence, with eternal pleasures at your right hand.
PSALM 16:11

Eternal pleasures are found at God's right hand.
Stop there. You don't have to look any further.
God places passions within you so that you'll keep
searching until you find utter delight in Him.

July 20

CHANGE THE THINGS YOU CAN

The Spirit of the LORD will come upon you in power . . .
and you will be changed into a different person. I SAMUEL 10:6

As the saying goes, God, give me the courage
to change the things I should. And give me the wisdom
to accept the things you don't want changed.

June 14

A SEAT AT THE BANQUET

A certain man was preparing a great banquet and invited many
guests. . . . But they all alike began to make excuses. . . .
Then the owner of the house became angry and ordered his servant,
"Go out quickly into the streets and alleys of the town and bring
in the poor, the crippled, the blind and the lame." LUKE 14:16-21

All you have to do is consider yourself a certified loser
and God will send His servant, Jesus,
to positively drag you into His house.

July 19

WHO'S IMPORTANT HERE?

When he heard that it was Jesus of Nazareth, he began to shout, "Jesus, Son of David, have mercy on me!" Many rebuked him and told him to be quiet, but he shouted all the more. MARK 10:47-48

Once these people understood that Jesus thought this poor handicapped person was important, once they realized the Lord's priorities, their whole attitude toward the obnoxious social outcast switched from negative to positive.

June 15

GRACE: GOD'S INITIATIVE

Then the master told his servant, "Go out to the roads and country
lanes and make them come in, so that my house will be full.
I tell you, not one of those men who were invited will get a taste
of my banquet." LUKE 14:23-24

God's grace is not a response to what men do.
God's grace is a divine initiative which is totally
unconnected to how good (or bad) men are.

Father, thank you for sending your servant Jesus
to search for me, find me, and bring me to your banquet.

July 18

THE FORGETFULNESS OF GOD

Remember not the sins of my youth and my rebellious ways;
according to your love remember me, for you are good, O LORD.
PSALM 25:7

Lord, my sins are lost somewhere in an unreachable sea.
You are greatly to be praised for such an act of sovereign
forgetfulness. Keep Satan from bringing to mind
my transgression through the impression
of sin that I see in my life.

June 16

TRUST

The disciples woke him and said to him,
"Teacher, don't you care if we drown?" MARK 4:38

May my trust in you be complete, O Lord.
May my confidence never waver and my hope
never falter. When stormy trials beset me,
may I rely on you finally and fully.

July 17

THE FAITHFUL GOD

Know therefore that the LORD your God is God; he is the faithful God, keeping his covenant of love to a thousand generations of those who love him and keep his commands. DEUTERONOMY 7:9

We are so prone to let our circumstances—whether good or bad—dictate our view of God. But time and again the Bible tells us that God is faithful. He is not just *a* faithful God, but *the* faithful God. He is the same steadfast and good Father yesterday, today, and forever.

June 17

ALL IS WELL

My heart says of you, "Seek His face!"
Your face, LORD, I will seek. PSALM 27:8

When the Spirit of Christ whispers to your troubled
heart, "*Seek His face*," don't delay. This is what is called
a prompting or a nudging of the Spirit. Seek Him
in His Word and through prayer. The peace that passes
all understanding will be yours when you hear
Him whisper, in return, "All is well."

July 16

MAKING HAY

The harvest is plentiful but the workers are few. Ask the Lord
of the harvest, therefore, to send out workers into his harvest field.
MATTHEW 9:37-38

Lord, grant me a measure of urgency and even panic
at the thought of the harvest. There are so many people
to reach. I pray for myself as a haymaker. And I pray
for others to join me that the crops be brought in on time.

June 18

THE BREAD OF ADVERSITY

Although the Lord gives you the bread of adversity and the water
of affliction, your teachers will be hidden no more;
with your own eyes you will see them. ISAIAH 30:20

Refining. Sifting. Pruning. Polishing. God gives you
the bread of adversity and the water of affliction
for good reasons. With God's Word as your teacher,
your own eyes can see the purpose of the Lord.

July 15

RESTITUTION

Be glad, O people of Zion, rejoice in the LORD your God . . .
"I will repay you for the years the locusts have eaten." JOEL 2:23,25

The Lord promises my losses shall be repaired.
He will make good on the damage I've done.
And like the father who more than made up for all
that his prodigal son had squandered,
God vows He will restore our loss.
That's what restitution is all about.

June 19

THE CLEAN AIR OF PRAYER

They all plotted together to come and fight against Jerusalem and stir up trouble against it. But we prayed to our God and posted a guard day and night to meet this threat. NEHEMIAH 4:8-9

Lord, when the Devil breathes threats, teach me to breathe your words in prayer. Teach me fresh conversation with you as something to be prized above all else. Thank you for hearing me and answering me.

July 14

SHORTWAVE PRAYING

For the LORD takes delight in His people . . . let the saints rejoice
in this honor and sing for joy on their beds. May the praise
of God be in their mouths and a double-edged sword
in their hands . . . PSALM 149:4-6

Lord, the world is smaller than I realize
and my prayers, go further than I imagine.
Even though my intercessions for others seem so faint,
thank you for amplifying prayer with your power.

June 20

WHO ARE THE ELECT?

For if you possess these qualities in increasing measure, they will keep you from being ineffective and unproductive in your knowledge of our Lord Jesus Christ. . . . Therefore, my brothers, be all the more eager to make your calling and election sure. For if you do these things, you will never fall, and you will receive a rich welcome into the eternal kingdom of our Lord and Savior Jesus Christ. II PETER 1:8,10-11

A changed life is the best evidence
that we are heading for heaven.

July 13

LEARNING HUMILITY

He guides the humble in what is right and teaches them his way.
PSALM 25:9

I praise you, Lord, for the marvelous grace
which sustains brothers and sisters who suffer greatly.
May we learn to see our own "handicaps"
as opportunities to humble ourselves
so that you might lift us up.

June 21

THIRST QUENCHER

My soul thirsts for God, for the living God.
PSALM 42:2

You may think that you have to actually crave God
before you come to Him. No. Express your cravings
to Him and expect Him to be the one
who will fulfill you, and you know what? He will.

July 12

A TASTE OF HELL

But the subjects of the kingdom will be thrown outside,
into the darkness, where there will be weeping and gnashing of teeth.
MATTHEW 8:12

There's nothing you could possibly be put through
on earth that can even begin to feel like the real hell.
So every time you think circumstances are hellish,
breathe a sigh of relief that Jesus has saved you
from the real thing.

June 22

LIFE IS HARD

We sent Timothy . . . to strengthen and encourage you in your faith, so that no one would be unsettled by these trials. You know quite well that we were destined for them. I THESSALONIANS 3:2-3

Life is a series of problems to be solved. Yes, solving problems is a painful process, but it is this whole process that gives our life meaning. So be strengthened and encouraged in your faith. Don't be unsettled by your trials. Trials are not for our pleasure; they are for our profit. Once you accept this truth, you transcend it. Once you truly know that life is difficult, then life is difficult no longer.

July 11

God-Watching

On my bed I remember you;
I think of you through the watches of the night. PSALM 63:6

I enjoy looking at people, thinking about where they
live, wondering where they work, and if they're happy.
Studying people, for me, is a habit.

Wouldn't it be great if we were as conscious about
studying God as we were people. Watching Him,
wondering about Him, looking closely at what makes
Him who He is, and just . . . enjoying Him.

June 23

LONGINGS

Instead, they were longing for a better country—a heavenly one.
Therefore God is not ashamed to be called their God,
for he has prepared a city for them. HEBREWS 11:16

Blessed Lord, my soul longs after you! Wrap my life
in your divine love and keep me ever desiring you.
Keep my heart from wandering away
and may I never lose sight of my heavenly home.

July 10

I Want to Go Home

But in keeping with his promise we are looking forward
to a new heaven and a new earth, the home of righteousness.
II Peter 3:13

"Home is where your heart is."
Never was a saying more true.
For when Jesus captures your heart,
you are then able to look forward
to your home of righteousness.

June 24

AT WAR WITH SPIRITS

Put on the full armor of God so that you can take your stand against the devil's schemes. EPHESIANS 6:11

Emotional fervor and tirades against the kingdom of Satan will not protect you. You would be talking to the wrong people. Talk instead with God. Listen to God. Demons scatter at such conversation.

July 9

THE SCHOOL OF OBEDIENCE

Although he was a son, he learned obedience from what he suffered and, once made perfect, he became the source of eternal salvation for all who obey him. HEBREWS 5:8-9

At times we may be like the young boy who, when disciplined by his father, complains, "He's making me suffer because he doesn't want me having any fun!" Actually, what God is doing is getting our minds off the toys and games of this world and teaching us tough obedience in preparation for the next.

June 25

A Heart That Won't Quit

Let us not become weary in doing good, for at the proper time
we will reap a harvest if we do not give up. GALATIANS 6:9

Don't let your heart quit.
For at the proper time we will reap!

Lord, when my heart gets tired and my soul gets weary,
strengthen me with your grace.

July 8

GUARD YOUR WORDS

Set a guard over my mouth, O LORD;
keep watch over the door of my lips. PSALM 141:3

Your mind, will and emotions are dangerously exposed
to ruin when you say things with an impure
or hurtful motive. So before you speak, ask yourself,
"Will what I say hurt or help? Will it glorify God?
Would I be ashamed if others heard?"

June 26

LANGUAGE OF LOVE

This is how we know what love is: Jesus Christ laid down his life for us. And we ought to lay down our lives for our brothers. I JOHN 3:16

Jesus could never, would never lay His life down
devoid of feeling or empty of emotion. To love
to the point of death is passion with a capital P!
Talk about love that is fervent and spirited!

And here's the point of today's reading:
This is the way we are to love our brothers and sisters.

July 7

WHAT A FRIEND

I no longer call you servants . . . I have called you friends,
for everything that I learned from my Father
I have made known to you. JOHN 15:15

Too often we stay at an arm's-length distance,
pulling back from the full intensity of an intimate
friendship with the Lord. We satisfy ourselves
with "less" when it comes to our relationship with Him.
But His love explodes our selfishness when we hear
Him say, "I have called you friends." His love breaks
our hearts as only an intimate friend can.

June 27

VIVE LA DIFFERENCE!

The LORD God said, "It is not good for the man to be alone.
I will make a helper suitable for him." GENESIS 2:18

The role of men and women in ministry
is complimentary. True enrichment for both Christian
men and women comes when these roles are being
fulfilled side by side. The church has too much to do
without squabbling about differences. Let's enjoy
our different roles and get on with ministry!

July 6

JESUS . . . AFTER THE ANGER

The blind and the lame came to him at the temple,
and he healed them. MATTHEW 21:14

These several verses paint a stunning picture
of our Savior. In both cases, Jesus was meeting the need
of the moment. In one verse it involved squaring off
against sin. The next verse, ministering to hurting people
who stood nearby. Either response requires
the resources of fearlessness and courage. Christ
could never be accused of being one-dimensional.

June 28

THE AFRICAN QUEEN

The Queen of the South will rise at the judgment with this generation
and condemn it; for she came from the ends of the earth to listen
to Solomon's wisdom, and now one greater than Solomon is here.
MATTHEW 12:42

If you have serious questions about God, His ways
and His will, don't sit on your curiosity. Let your thirst
for God take you on a journey of questioning. It's okay
to have doubts and to wrestle with spiritual issues. And
like the Queen of Sheba, who left Israel fully satisfied,
God delights in giving answers to our hardest questions.

July 5

JESUS ... TAKING A STAND

Jesus entered the temple area and drove out all who were buying
and selling there. He overturned the tables of the money changers
and the benches of those selling doves. MATTHEW 21:12

Friend of Sinners, don't be gentle with any sin
that I might be safeguarding in my life. Expose
the dark recesses in my heart, square off
against my sin and uproot it out of my life.

June 29

GOD SINGS

The LORD your God is with you, he is mighty to save. He will take great delight in you, he will quiet you with his love, he will rejoice over you with singing. ZEPHANIAH 3:17

Put a song in my heart today, Lord, a praise song or a hymn that you wish to sing to me. May I enjoy your melody and may I remember throughout the day that it is your song. It is your singing. My, you sing beautifully!

July 4

NOT ONE RAY OF LIGHT

Let him who walks in the dark, who has no light,
trust in the name of the LORD and rely on his God. ISAIAH 50:10

You probably have days that seem like deep,
cavernous holes. Days when you can't find your way
because of the darkness. You search for a single ray
of light and see absolutely nothing.

Don't be alarmed. Remember that your walk
is not by sight, but by faith.

July 2

THE PEOPLE YOU DISLIKE

Do nothing out of selfish ambition or vain conceit, but in humility consider others better than yourselves. PHILIPPIANS 2:3

Deep and abiding devotion to Jesus will give you a new perspective on people you dislike. Affection for God that is warm and heartfelt will give boundless joy in difficult relationships. Fervent love for the Lord will give you love for needy people. Love God, and you can't help but love people.

July 1

GOD WITH A WASH CLOTH

Cleanse me with hyssop, and I will be clean; wash me,
and I will be whiter than snow. PSALM 51:7

Almighty God, thank you for desiring to make me
clean. For washing me of my sins, cleansing my heart
and making me pure. I humble myself before you
and present all the areas of my life that need to be made
right. I'm grateful that you desire to do something so
powerful and personal in my life as to make me spotless
and stainless. Thank you for shedding your blood
on the cross, your blood that washes me white as snow.

July 3

HE DELIGHTS OVER YOU

The LORD will take delight in you. . . . As a bridegroom rejoices
over his bride, so will your God rejoice over you. ISAIAH 62:4-5

God takes great delight in you. You give Him great joy.
He finds pleasure and satisfaction in your worship
and praise. And your obedience brings a smile
to His face. Love Him today with all your heart.
After all, every day His heart is full of love for you.

June 30

FAITH THAT PLEASES

And without faith it is impossible to please God. HEBREWS 11:6

Faith means being sure of Christ's commitment
to you, rather than your commitment to Him.
Faith is having confidence in His love for you
rather than your love for Him.

So if you want to place your faith in Christ,
surrender all, everything to Him.
This is faith that pleases God.